MW01078895

The Law School Admission Council (LSAC) is a nonprofit corporation whose members are more than 200 law schools in the United States, Canada, and Australia. Headquartered in Newtown, PA, USA, the Council was founded in 1947 to facilitate the law school admission process. The Council has grown to provide numerous products and services to law schools and to approximately 85,000 law school applicants each year.

All law schools approved by the American Bar Association (ABA) are LSAC members. Canadian law schools recognized by a provincial or territorial law society or government agency are also members. Accredited law schools outside of the United States and Canada are eligible for membership at the discretion of the LSAC Board of Trustees; Melbourne Law School, the University of Melbourne is the first LSAC-member law school outside of North America.

The services provided by LSAC are the Law School Admission Test (LSAT); the Credential Assembly Service, which includes letters of recommendation, electronic applications, and domestic and international transcript processing for JD degrees; the LLM Credential Assembly Service; the Candidate Referral Service (CRS); the Admission Communication & Exchange System (ACES, ACES²); research and statistical reports; websites for law schools and prelaw advisors (*LSACnet.org*), law school applicants (*LSAC.org*), and undergraduates from minority groups (*DiscoverLaw.org*); testing and admission-related consultations with legal educators worldwide; and various publications, videos, and LSAT preparation tools. LSAC does not engage in assessing an applicant's chances for admission to any law school; all admission decisions are made by individual law schools.

LSAT, *The Official LSAT PrepTest, The Official LSAT SuperPrep, ItemWise,* and LSAC are registered marks of the Law School Admission Council, Inc. Law School Forums and LSAC Credential Assembly Service are service marks of the Law School Admission Council, Inc. *10 Actual, Official LSAT PrepTests; 10 More Actual, Official LSAT PrepTests; The Next 10 Actual, Official LSAT PrepTests; The New Whole Law School Package; ABA-LSAC Official Guide to ABA-Approved Law Schools; Whole Test Prep Packages;* LSDAS; LLM Credential Assembly Service; ACES²; ADMIT-LLM; *LSACnet;* Law School Admission Test; and Law School Admission Council are trademarks of the Law School Admission Council, Inc.

LSAC fees, policies, and procedures relating to, but not limited to, test registration, test administration, test score reporting, misconduct and irregularities, Credential Assembly Service (CAS), and other matters may change without notice at any time. Up-to-date LSAC policies and procedures are available at *www.LSAC.org*, or you may contact our candidate service representatives.

ISBN-13: 978-0-9793050-8-5
ISBN-10: 0-9793050-8-X

Print number
10 9 8 7 6 5 4 3 2

Table of Contents

The Law School Admission Test is a half-day standardized test required for admission to all ABA-approved law schools, most Canadian law schools, and many non-ABA-approved law schools. It consists of five 35-minute sections of multiple-choice questions. Four of the five sections contribute to the test taker's score. These sections include one reading comprehension section, one analytical reasoning section, and two logical reasoning sections. The unscored section, commonly referred to as the variable section, typically is used to pretest new test questions or to preequate new test forms. The placement of this section in the LSAT will vary. A 35-minute writing sample is administered at the end of the test. The writing sample is not scored by LSAC, but copies are sent to all law schools to which you apply. The score scale for the LSAT is 120 to 180.

The LSAT is designed to measure skills considered essential for success in law school: the reading and comprehension of complex texts with accuracy and insight; the organization and management of information and the ability to draw reasonable inferences from it; the ability to think critically; and the analysis and evaluation of the reasoning and arguments of others.

The LSAT provides a standard measure of acquired reading and verbal reasoning skills that law schools can use as one of several factors in assessing applicants.

For up-to-date information about LSAC's services, go to our website, *www.LSAC.org*.

Scoring

Your LSAT score is based on the number of questions you answer correctly (the raw score). There is no deduction for incorrect answers, and all questions count equally. In other words, there is no penalty for guessing.

■ Test Score Accuracy—Reliability and Standard Error of Measurement

Candidates perform at different levels on different occasions for reasons quite unrelated to the characteristics of a test itself. The accuracy of test scores is best described by the use of two related statistical terms: reliability and standard error of measurement.

Reliability is a measure of how consistently a test measures the skills being assessed. The higher the reliability coefficient for a test, the more certain we can be that test takers would get very similar scores if they took the test again.

LSAC reports an internal consistency measure of reliability for every test form. Reliability can vary from 0.00 to 1.00, and a test with no measurement error would have a reliability coefficient of 1.00 (never attained in practice). Reliability coefficients for past LSAT forms have ranged from .90 to .95, indicating a high degree of consistency for these tests. LSAC expects the reliability of the LSAT to continue to fall within the same range.

LSAC also reports the amount of measurement error associated with each test form, a concept known as the standard error of measurement (SEM). The SEM, which is usually about 2.6 points, indicates how close a test taker's observed score is likely to be to his or her true score. True scores are theoretical scores that would be obtained from perfectly reliable tests with no measurement error—scores never known in practice.

Score bands, or ranges of scores that contain a test taker's true score a certain percentage of the time, can be derived using the SEM. LSAT score bands are constructed by adding and subtracting the (rounded)

SEM to and from an actual LSAT score (e.g., the LSAT score, plus or minus 3 points). Scores near 120 or 180 have asymmetrical bands. Score bands constructed in this manner will contain an individual's true score approximately 68 percent of the time.

Measurement error also must be taken into account when comparing LSAT scores of two test takers. It is likely that small differences in scores are due to measurement error rather than to meaningful differences in ability. The standard error of score differences provides some guidance as to the importance of differences between two scores. The standard error of score differences is approximately 1.4 times larger than the standard error of measurement for the individual scores.

Thus, a test score should be regarded as a useful but approximate measure of a test taker's abilities as measured by the test, not as an exact determination of his or her abilities. LSAC encourages law schools to examine the range of scores within the interval that probably contains the test taker's true score (e.g., the test taker's score band) rather than solely interpret the reported score alone.

■ Adjustments for Variation in Test Difficulty

All test forms of the LSAT reported on the same score scale are designed to measure the same abilities, but one test form may be slightly easier or more difficult than another. The scores from different test forms are made comparable through a statistical procedure known as equating. As a result of equating, a given scaled score earned on different test forms reflects the same level of ability.

■ Research on the LSAT

Summaries of LSAT validity studies and other LSAT research can be found in member law school libraries.

■ **To Inquire About Test Questions**

If you find what you believe to be an error or ambiguity in a test question that affects your response to the question, contact LSAC by e-mail: *LSATTS@LSAC.org*, or write to Law School Admission Council, Test Development Group, Box 40, Newtown, PA 18940-0040.

How This PrepTest Differs From an Actual LSAT

This PrepTest is made up of the scored sections and writing sample from the actual disclosed LSAT administered in October 2008. However, it does not contain the extra, variable section that is used to pretest new test items of one of the three multiple-choice question types. The three multiple-choice question types may be in a different order in an actual LSAT than in this PrepTest. This is because the order of these question types is intentionally varied for each administration of the test.

The Question Types

The multiple-choice questions that make up most of the LSAT reflect a broad range of academic disciplines and are intended to give no advantage to candidates from a particular academic background.

The five sections of the test contain three different question types. The following material presents a general discussion of the nature of each question type and some strategies that can be used in answering them.

■ **Analytical Reasoning Questions**

Analytical reasoning items are designed to measure your ability to understand a structure of relationships and to draw logical conclusions about the structure. You are asked to make deductions from a set of statements, rules, or conditions that describe relationships among entities such as persons, places, things, or events. They simulate the kinds of detailed analyses of relationships that a law student must perform in solving legal problems. For example, a passage might describe four diplomats sitting around a table, following certain rules of protocol as to who can sit where. You must answer questions about the implications of the given information, for example, who is sitting between diplomats X and Y.

The passage used for each group of questions describes a common relationship such as the following:

- Assignment: Two parents, P and O, and their children, R and S, must go to the dentist on four consecutive days, designated 1, 2, 3, and 4;

- Ordering: X arrived before Y but after Z;

- Grouping: A manager is trying to form a project team from seven staff members—R, S, T, U, V, W, and X. Each staff member has a particular strength—writing, planning, or facilitating;

- Spatial: A certain country contains six cities and each city is connected to at least one other city by a system of roads, some of which are one-way.

Careful reading and analysis are necessary to determine the exact nature of the relationships involved. Some relationships are fixed (e.g., P and R always sit at the same table). Other relationships are variable (e.g., Q must be assigned to either table 1 or table 3). Some relationships that are not stated in the conditions are implied by and can be deduced from those that are stated. (e.g., If one condition about books on a shelf specifies that Book L is to the left of Book Y, and another specifies that Book P is to the left of Book L, then it can be deduced that Book P is to the left of Book Y.)

No formal training in logic is required to answer these questions correctly. Analytical reasoning questions are intended to be answered using knowledge, skills, and reasoning ability generally expected of college students and graduates.

Suggested Approach

Some people may prefer to answer first those questions about a passage that seem less difficult and then those that seem more difficult. In general, it is best not to start another passage before finishing one begun earlier, because much time can be lost in returning to a passage and reestablishing familiarity with its relationships. Do not assume that, because the conditions for a set of questions look long or complicated, the questions based on those conditions will necessarily be especially difficult.

Reading the passage. In reading the conditions, do not introduce unwarranted assumptions. For instance, in a set establishing relationships of height and weight among the members of a team, do not assume that a person who is taller than another person must weigh more than that person. All the information needed to answer each question is provided in the passage and the question itself.

The conditions are designed to be as clear as possible; do not interpret them as if they were intended to trick you. For example, if a question asks how many people could be eligible to serve on a committee, consider only those people named in the passage unless directed otherwise. When in doubt, read the conditions in their most obvious sense. Remember, however, that the language in the conditions is intended to be read for precise meaning. It is essential to pay particular attention to words that describe or limit relationships, such as "only," "exactly," "never," "always," "must be," "cannot be," and the like.

The result of this careful reading will be a clear picture of the structure of the relationships involved, including the kinds of relationships permitted, the participants in the relationships, and the range of actions or attributes allowed by the relationships for these participants.

Questions are independent. Each question should be considered separately from the other questions in its set; no information, except what is given in the original conditions, should be carried over from one question to another. In some cases a question will simply ask for conclusions to be drawn from the conditions as originally given. Some questions may, however, add information to the original conditions or temporarily suspend one of the original conditions for the purpose of that question only. For example, if Question 1 adds the information "if P is sitting at table 2 ...," this information should NOT be carried over to any other question in the group.

Highlighting the text; using diagrams. Many people find it useful to underline key points in the passage and in each question. In addition, it may prove very helpful to draw a diagram to assist you in finding the solution to the problem.

In preparing for the test, you may wish to experiment with different types of diagrams. For a scheduling problem, a calendar-like diagram may be helpful. For a spatial relationship problem, a simple map can be a useful device.

Even though some people find diagrams to be very helpful, other people seldom use them. And among those who do regularly use diagrams in solving these problems, there is by no means universal agreement on which kind of diagram is best for which problem or in which cases a diagram is most useful. Do not be concerned if a particular problem in the test seems to be best approached without the use of a diagram.

■ Logical Reasoning Questions

Logical reasoning questions evaluate your ability to understand, analyze, criticize, and complete a variety of arguments. The arguments are contained in short passages taken from a variety of sources, including letters to the editor, speeches, advertisements, newspaper articles and editorials, informal discussions and conversations, as well as articles in the humanities, the social sciences, and the natural sciences.

Each logical reasoning question requires you to read and comprehend a short passage, then answer one or two questions about it. The questions test a variety of abilities involved in reasoning logically and thinking critically. These include:

- recognizing the point or issue of an argument or dispute;

- detecting the assumptions involved in an argumentation or chain of reasoning;

- drawing reasonable conclusions from given evidence or premises;

- identifying and applying principles;

- identifying the method or structure of an argument or chain of reasoning;

- detecting reasoning errors and misinterpretations;

- determining how additional evidence or argumentation affects an argument or conclusion; and

- identifying explanations and recognizing resolutions of conflicting facts or arguments.

The questions do not presuppose knowledge of the terminology of formal logic. For example, you will not be expected to know the meaning of specialized terms such as "ad hominem" or "syllogism." On the other hand, you will be expected to understand and critique the reasoning contained in arguments. This requires that you possess, at a minimum, a college-level understanding of widely used concepts such as argument, premise, assumption, and conclusion.

Suggested Approach

Read each question carefully. Make sure that you understand the meaning of each part of the question. Make sure that you understand the meaning of each answer choice and the ways in which it may or may not relate to the question posed.

Do not pick a response simply because it is a true statement. Although true, it may not answer the question posed.

Answer each question on the basis of the information that is given, even if you do not agree with it. Work within the context provided by the passage. LSAT questions do not involve any tricks or hidden meanings.

■ Reading Comprehension Questions

The purpose of reading comprehension questions is to measure your ability to read, with understanding and insight, examples of lengthy and complex materials similar to those commonly encountered in law school work. The reading comprehension section of the LSAT contains four sets of reading questions, each consisting of a selection of reading material followed by five to eight questions. The reading selection in three of the four sets consists of a single reading passage of approximately 450 words in length. The other set contains two related shorter passages. Sets with two passages are a new variant of reading comprehension, called comparative reading, which were introduced into the reading comprehension section in June 2007. See "Comparative Reading" below for more information.

Reading selections for reading comprehension questions are drawn from subjects such as the humanities, the social sciences, the biological and physical sciences, and issues related to the law. Reading comprehension questions require you to read carefully and accurately, to determine the relationships among the various parts of the reading selection, and to draw reasonable inferences from the material in the selection. The questions may ask about the following characteristics of a passage or pair of passages:

- the main idea or primary purpose;

- the meaning or purpose of words or phrases used;

- information explicitly stated;

- information or ideas that can be inferred;

- the organization or structure;

- the application of information in a passage to a new context; and

- the author's attitude as it is revealed in the tone of a passage or the language used.

Suggested Approach

Since reading selections are drawn from many different disciplines and sources, you should not be discouraged if you encounter material with which you are not familiar. It is important to remember that questions are to be answered exclusively on the basis of the information provided in the selection. There is no particular knowledge that you are expected to bring to the test, and you should not make inferences based on any prior knowledge of a subject that you may have. You may, however, wish to defer working on a set of questions that seems particularly difficult or unfamiliar until after you have dealt with sets you find easier.

Strategies. In preparing for the test, you should experiment with different strategies and decide which work most effectively for you. These include:

- reading the selection very closely and then answering the questions;

- reading the questions first, reading the selection closely, and then returning to the questions; or

- skimming the selection and questions very quickly, then rereading the selection closely and answering the questions.

Remember that your strategy must be effective for you under timed conditions.

Reading the selection. Whatever strategy you choose, you should give the passage or pair of passages at least one careful reading before answering the questions. Try to distinguish main ideas from supporting ideas, and opinions or attitudes from factual, objective information. Note transitions from one idea to the next and examine the relationships among the different ideas or parts of a passage, or between the two passages in comparative reading sets. Consider how and why an author makes points and draws conclusions. Be sensitive to implications of what the passages say.

You may find it helpful to mark key parts of passages. For example, you might underline main ideas or important arguments, and you might circle transitional words—"although," "nevertheless," "correspondingly," and the like—that will help you map the structure of a passage. Moreover, you might note descriptive words that will help you identify an author's attitude toward a particular idea or person.

Answering the Questions

- Always read all the answer choices before selecting the best answer. The best answer choice is the one that most accurately and completely answers the question being posed.

- Respond to the specific question being asked. Do not pick an answer choice simply because it is a true statement. For example, picking a true statement might yield an incorrect answer to a question in which you are asked to identify an author's position on an issue, since here you are not being asked to evaluate the truth of the author's position but only to correctly identify what that position is.

- Answer the questions only on the basis of the information provided in the selection. Your own views, interpretations, or opinions, and those you have heard from others, may sometimes conflict with those expressed in a reading selection; however, you are expected to work within the context provided by the reading selection. You should not expect to agree with everything you encounter in reading comprehension passages.

■ Comparative Reading

As of the June 2007 administration, LSAC introduced a new variant of reading comprehension, called comparative reading, as one of the four sets in the LSAT reading comprehension section. In general, comparative reading questions are similar to traditional reading comprehension questions, except that comparative reading questions are based on two shorter passages instead of one longer passage. The two passages together are of roughly the same length as one reading comprehension passage, so the total amount of reading in the reading comprehension section remains essentially the same. A few of the questions that follow a comparative reading passage pair might concern only one of the two passages, but most will be about both passages and how they relate to each other.

Comparative reading questions reflect the nature of some important tasks in law school work, such as understanding arguments from multiple texts by applying skills of comparison, contrast, generalization, and synthesis to the texts. The purpose of comparative reading is to assess this important set of skills directly.

What Comparative Reading Looks Like

The two passages in a comparative reading set—labeled **"Passage A"** and **"Passage B"**—discuss the same topic or related topics. The topics fall into the same academic categories traditionally used in reading comprehension: humanities, natural sciences, social sciences, and issues related to the law. Like traditional reading comprehension passages, comparative reading passages are complex and generally involve argument. The two passages in a comparative reading pair are typically adapted from two different published sources written by two different authors. They are usually independent of each other, with neither author responding directly to the other.

As you read the pair of passages, it is helpful to try to determine what the central idea or main point of each passage is, and to determine how the passages relate to each other. The passages will relate to each other in various ways. In some cases, the authors of the passages will be in general agreement with each other, while in others their views will be directly opposed. Passage pairs may also exhibit more complex types of relationships: for example, one passage might articulate a set of principles, while the other passage applies those or similar principles to a particular situation.

Questions that are concerned with only one of the passages are essentially identical to traditional reading comprehension questions. Questions that address both passages test the same fundamental reading skills as traditional reading comprehension questions, but the skills are applied to two texts instead of one. You may be asked to identify a main purpose shared by both passages, a statement with which both authors would agree, or a similarity or dissimilarity in the structure of the arguments in the two passages. The following are additional examples of comparative reading questions:

- Which one of the following is the central topic of each passage?

- Both passages explicitly mention which one of the following?

- Which one of the following statements is most strongly supported by both passages?

- Which one of the following most accurately describes the attitude expressed by the author of passage B toward the overall argument in passage A?

- The relationship between passage A and passage B is most analogous to the relationship in which one of the following?

This is not a complete list of the sorts of questions you may be asked in a comparative reading set, but it illustrates the range of questions you may be asked.

The Writing Sample

On the day of the test, you will be asked to write one sample essay. LSAC does not score the writing sample, but copies are sent to all law schools to which you apply. According to a 2006 LSAC survey of 157 United States and Canadian law schools, almost all utilize the writing sample in evaluating some applications for admission. Frivolous responses or no responses to writing sample prompts have been used by law schools as grounds for rejection of applications for admission.

In developing and implementing the writing sample portion of the LSAT, LSAC has operated on the following premises: First, law schools and the legal profession value highly the ability to communicate effectively in writing. Second, it is important to encourage potential law students to develop effective writing skills. Third, a sample of an applicant's writing, produced under controlled conditions, is a potentially useful indication of that

person's writing ability. Fourth, the writing sample can serve as an independent check on other writing submitted by applicants as part of the admission process. Finally, writing samples may be useful for diagnostic purposes.

You will have 35 minutes in which to plan and write an essay on the topic you receive. Read the topic and the accompanying directions carefully. You will probably find it best to spend a few minutes considering the topic and organizing your thoughts before you begin writing. In your essay, be sure to develop your ideas fully, leaving time, if possible, to review what you have written. Do not write on a topic other than the one specified. Writing on a topic of your own choice is not acceptable.

No special knowledge is required or expected for this writing exercise. Law schools are interested in the reasoning, clarity, organization, language usage, and writing mechanics displayed in your essay. How well you write is more important than how much you write. Confine your essay to the blocked, lined area on the front and back of the Writing Sample Response Sheet. Only that area will be reproduced for law schools. Be sure that your writing is legible.

The writing prompt presents a decision problem. You are asked to make a choice between two positions or courses of action. Both of the choices are defensible, and you are given criteria and facts on which to base your decision. There is no "right" or "wrong" position to take on the topic, so the quality of each test taker's response is a function not of which choice is made, but of how well or poorly the choice is supported and how well or poorly the other choice is criticized.

Taking the PrepTest Under Simulated LSAT Conditions

One important way to prepare for the LSAT is to simulate the day of the test by taking a practice test under actual time constraints. Taking a practice test under timed conditions helps you to estimate the amount of time you can afford to spend on each question in a section and to determine the question types on which you may need additional practice.

Since the LSAT is a timed test, it is important to use your allotted time wisely. During the test, you may work only on the section designated by the test supervisor. You cannot devote extra time to a difficult section and make up that time on a section you find easier. In pacing yourself, and checking your answers, you should think of each section of the test as a separate minitest.

Be sure that you answer every question on the test. When you do not know the correct answer to a question, first eliminate the responses that you know are incorrect, then make your best guess among the remaining choices. Do not be afraid to guess as there is no penalty for incorrect answers.

When you take a practice test, abide by all the requirements specified in the directions and keep strictly within the specified time limits. Work without a rest period. When you take an actual test, you will have only a short break—usually 10-15 minutes—after SECTION III. When taken under conditions as much like actual testing conditions as possible, a practice test provides very useful preparation for taking the LSAT.

Official directions for the four multiple-choice sections and the writing sample are included in this PrepTest so that you can approximate actual testing conditions as you practice.

To take the test:

- Set a timer for 35 minutes. Answer all the questions in SECTION I of this PrepTest. Stop working on that section when the 35 minutes have elapsed.

- Repeat, allowing yourself 35 minutes each for sections II, III, and IV.

- Set the timer again for 35 minutes, then prepare your response to the writing sample topic at the end of this PrepTest.

- Refer to "Computing Your Score" for the PrepTest for instruction on evaluating your performance. An answer key is provided for that purpose.

The practice test that follows consists of four sections corresponding to the four scored sections of the October 2008 LSAT. Also reprinted is the October 2008 unscored writing sample topic.

General Directions for the LSAT Answer Sheet

The actual testing time for this portion of the test will be 2 hours 55 minutes. There are five sections, each with a time limit of 35 minutes. The supervisor will tell you when to begin and end each section. If you finish a section before time is called, you may check your work on that section only; do not turn to any other section of the test book and do not work on any other section either in the test book or on the answer sheet.

There are several different types of questions on the test, and each question type has its own directions. Be sure you understand the directions for each question type before attempting to answer any questions in that section.

Not everyone will finish all the questions in the time allowed. Do not hurry, but work steadily and as quickly as you can without sacrificing accuracy. You are advised to use your time effectively. If a question seems too difficult, go on to the next one and return to the difficult question after completing the section. MARK THE BEST ANSWER YOU CAN FOR EVERY QUESTION. NO DEDUCTIONS WILL BE MADE FOR WRONG ANSWERS. YOUR SCORE WILL BE BASED ONLY ON THE NUMBER OF QUESTIONS YOU ANSWER CORRECTLY.

ALL YOUR ANSWERS MUST BE MARKED ON THE ANSWER SHEET. Answer spaces for each question are lettered to correspond with the letters of the potential answers to each question in the test book. After you have decided which of the answers is correct, blacken the corresponding space on the answer sheet. BE SURE THAT EACH MARK IS BLACK AND COMPLETELY FILLS THE ANSWER SPACE. Give only one answer to each question. If you change an answer, be sure that all previous marks are erased completely. Since the answer sheet is machine scored, incomplete erasures may be interpreted as intended answers. ANSWERS RECORDED IN THE TEST BOOK WILL NOT BE SCORED.

There may be more questions noted on this answer sheet than there are questions in a section. Do not be concerned but be certain that the section and number of the question you are answering matches the answer sheet section and question number. Additional answer spaces in any answer sheet section should be left blank. Begin your next section in the number one answer space for that section.

LSAC takes various steps to ensure that answer sheets are returned from test centers in a timely manner for processing. In the unlikely event that an answer sheet(s) is not received, LSAC will permit the examinee to either retest at no additional fee or to receive a refund of his or her LSAT fee. THESE REMEDIES ARE THE EXCLUSIVE REMEDIES AVAILABLE IN THE UNLIKELY EVENT THAT AN ANSWER SHEET IS NOT RECEIVED BY LSAC.

Score Cancellation

Complete this section only if you are absolutely certain you want to cancel your score. A CANCELLATION REQUEST CANNOT BE RESCINDED. IF YOU ARE AT ALL UNCERTAIN, YOU SHOULD NOT COMPLETE THIS SECTION.

To cancel your score from this administration, you must:

A. fill in both ovals here ..... ⚪⚪
              AND

B. read the following statement. Then sign your name and enter the date.
   YOUR SIGNATURE ALONE IS NOT SUFFICIENT FOR SCORE CANCELLATION. BOTH OVALS ABOVE MUST BE FILLED IN FOR SCANNING EQUIPMENT TO RECOGNIZE YOUR REQUEST FOR SCORE CANCELLATION.

   I certify that I wish to cancel my test score from this administration. I understand that my request is irreversible and that my score will not be sent to me or to the law schools to which I apply.

_____
Sign your name in full

_____
Date

HOW DID YOU PREPARE FOR THE LSAT?
(Select all that apply.)

Responses to this item are voluntary and will be used for statistical research purposes only.

- ⚪ By studying the sample questions in the *LSAT & LSDAS Information Book.*
- ⚪ By taking the free sample LSAT in the *LSAT & LSDAS Information Book.*
- ⚪ By working through official LSAT *PrepTests, ItemWise,* and/or other LSAC test prep products.
- ⚪ By using LSAT prep books or software not published by LSAC.
- ⚪ By attending a commercial test preparation or coaching course.
- ⚪ By attending a test preparation or coaching course offered through an undergraduate institution.
- ⚪ Self study.
- ⚪ Other preparation.
- ⚪ No preparation.

CERTIFYING STATEMENT

Please write (DO NOT PRINT) the following statement. Sign and date.

I certify that I am the examinee whose name appears on this answer sheet and that I am here to take the LSAT for the sole purpose of being considered for admission to law school. I further certify that I will neither assist nor receive assistance from any other candidate, and I agree not to copy or retain examination questions or to transmit them to or discuss them with any other person in any form.

_____
_____
_____
_____
_____
_____
_____
_____
_____

SIGNATURE: _____   TODAY'S DATE: ___/___/___
                                                          MONTH DAY YEAR

INSTRUCTIONS FOR COMPLETING THE BIOGRAPHICAL AREA ARE ON THE BACK COVER OF YOUR TEST BOOKLET.
USE ONLY A NO. 2 OR HB PENCIL TO COMPLETE THIS ANSWER SHEET. DO NOT USE INK.

A

USE A NO. 2 OR HB PENCIL ONLY

● Right Mark   ⊘ ⊗ ◎ Wrong Marks

1 LAST NAME   FIRST NAME   MI

2 SOCIAL SECURITY/ SOCIAL INSURANCE NO.

3 LSAC ACCOUNT NUMBER

L

4 DATE OF BIRTH

MONTH	DAY	YEAR
○ Jan		
○ Feb		
○ Mar		
○ Apr		
○ May		
○ June		
○ July		
○ Aug		
○ Sept		
○ Oct		
○ Nov		
○ Dec		

5 RACIAL/ETHNIC DESCRIPTION
Mark one or more
○ 1 Aboriginal/TSI Australian
○ 2 Amer. Indian/Alaska Native
○ 3 Asian
○ 4 Black/African American
○ 5 Canadian Aboriginal
○ 6 Caucasian/White
○ 7 Hispanic/Latino
○ 8 Native Hawaiian/Other Pacific Islander
○ 9 Puerto Rican

6 GENDER
○ Male
○ Female

7 DOMINANT LANGUAGE
○ English
○ Other

8 ENGLISH FLUENCY
○ Yes   ○ No

9 TEST BOOK SERIAL NO.

10 TEST FORM

11 TEST DATE
MONTH   DAY   YEAR

12 CENTER NUMBER

13 TEST FORM CODE

Law School Admission Test

Mark one and only one answer to each question. Be sure to fill in completely the space for your intended answer choice. If you erase, do so completely. Make no stray marks.

SECTION 1

1 Ⓐ Ⓑ Ⓒ Ⓓ Ⓔ
2 Ⓐ Ⓑ Ⓒ Ⓓ Ⓔ
3 Ⓐ Ⓑ Ⓒ Ⓓ Ⓔ
4 Ⓐ Ⓑ Ⓒ Ⓓ Ⓔ
5 Ⓐ Ⓑ Ⓒ Ⓓ Ⓔ
6 Ⓐ Ⓑ Ⓒ Ⓓ Ⓔ
7 Ⓐ Ⓑ Ⓒ Ⓓ Ⓔ
8 Ⓐ Ⓑ Ⓒ Ⓓ Ⓔ
9 Ⓐ Ⓑ Ⓒ Ⓓ Ⓔ
10 Ⓐ Ⓑ Ⓒ Ⓓ Ⓔ
11 Ⓐ Ⓑ Ⓒ Ⓓ Ⓔ
12 Ⓐ Ⓑ Ⓒ Ⓓ Ⓔ
13 Ⓐ Ⓑ Ⓒ Ⓓ Ⓔ
14 Ⓐ Ⓑ Ⓒ Ⓓ Ⓔ
15 Ⓐ Ⓑ Ⓒ Ⓓ Ⓔ
16 Ⓐ Ⓑ Ⓒ Ⓓ Ⓔ
17 Ⓐ Ⓑ Ⓒ Ⓓ Ⓔ
18 Ⓐ Ⓑ Ⓒ Ⓓ Ⓔ
19 Ⓐ Ⓑ Ⓒ Ⓓ Ⓔ
20 Ⓐ Ⓑ Ⓒ Ⓓ Ⓔ
21 Ⓐ Ⓑ Ⓒ Ⓓ Ⓔ
22 Ⓐ Ⓑ Ⓒ Ⓓ Ⓔ
23 Ⓐ Ⓑ Ⓒ Ⓓ Ⓔ
24 Ⓐ Ⓑ Ⓒ Ⓓ Ⓔ
25 Ⓐ Ⓑ Ⓒ Ⓓ Ⓔ
26 Ⓐ Ⓑ Ⓒ Ⓓ Ⓔ
27 Ⓐ Ⓑ Ⓒ Ⓓ Ⓔ
28 Ⓐ Ⓑ Ⓒ Ⓓ Ⓔ
29 Ⓐ Ⓑ Ⓒ Ⓓ Ⓔ
30 Ⓐ Ⓑ Ⓒ Ⓓ Ⓔ

SECTION 2

1 Ⓐ Ⓑ Ⓒ Ⓓ Ⓔ
2 Ⓐ Ⓑ Ⓒ Ⓓ Ⓔ
3 Ⓐ Ⓑ Ⓒ Ⓓ Ⓔ
4 Ⓐ Ⓑ Ⓒ Ⓓ Ⓔ
5 Ⓐ Ⓑ Ⓒ Ⓓ Ⓔ
6 Ⓐ Ⓑ Ⓒ Ⓓ Ⓔ
7 Ⓐ Ⓑ Ⓒ Ⓓ Ⓔ
8 Ⓐ Ⓑ Ⓒ Ⓓ Ⓔ
9 Ⓐ Ⓑ Ⓒ Ⓓ Ⓔ
10 Ⓐ Ⓑ Ⓒ Ⓓ Ⓔ
11 Ⓐ Ⓑ Ⓒ Ⓓ Ⓔ
12 Ⓐ Ⓑ Ⓒ Ⓓ Ⓔ
13 Ⓐ Ⓑ Ⓒ Ⓓ Ⓔ
14 Ⓐ Ⓑ Ⓒ Ⓓ Ⓔ
15 Ⓐ Ⓑ Ⓒ Ⓓ Ⓔ
16 Ⓐ Ⓑ Ⓒ Ⓓ Ⓔ
17 Ⓐ Ⓑ Ⓒ Ⓓ Ⓔ
18 Ⓐ Ⓑ Ⓒ Ⓓ Ⓔ
19 Ⓐ Ⓑ Ⓒ Ⓓ Ⓔ
20 Ⓐ Ⓑ Ⓒ Ⓓ Ⓔ
21 Ⓐ Ⓑ Ⓒ Ⓓ Ⓔ
22 Ⓐ Ⓑ Ⓒ Ⓓ Ⓔ
23 Ⓐ Ⓑ Ⓒ Ⓓ Ⓔ
24 Ⓐ Ⓑ Ⓒ Ⓓ Ⓔ
25 Ⓐ Ⓑ Ⓒ Ⓓ Ⓔ
26 Ⓐ Ⓑ Ⓒ Ⓓ Ⓔ
27 Ⓐ Ⓑ Ⓒ Ⓓ Ⓔ
28 Ⓐ Ⓑ Ⓒ Ⓓ Ⓔ
29 Ⓐ Ⓑ Ⓒ Ⓓ Ⓔ
30 Ⓐ Ⓑ Ⓒ Ⓓ Ⓔ

SECTION 3

1 Ⓐ Ⓑ Ⓒ Ⓓ Ⓔ
2 Ⓐ Ⓑ Ⓒ Ⓓ Ⓔ
3 Ⓐ Ⓑ Ⓒ Ⓓ Ⓔ
4 Ⓐ Ⓑ Ⓒ Ⓓ Ⓔ
5 Ⓐ Ⓑ Ⓒ Ⓓ Ⓔ
6 Ⓐ Ⓑ Ⓒ Ⓓ Ⓔ
7 Ⓐ Ⓑ Ⓒ Ⓓ Ⓔ
8 Ⓐ Ⓑ Ⓒ Ⓓ Ⓔ
9 Ⓐ Ⓑ Ⓒ Ⓓ Ⓔ
10 Ⓐ Ⓑ Ⓒ Ⓓ Ⓔ
11 Ⓐ Ⓑ Ⓒ Ⓓ Ⓔ
12 Ⓐ Ⓑ Ⓒ Ⓓ Ⓔ
13 Ⓐ Ⓑ Ⓒ Ⓓ Ⓔ
14 Ⓐ Ⓑ Ⓒ Ⓓ Ⓔ
15 Ⓐ Ⓑ Ⓒ Ⓓ Ⓔ
16 Ⓐ Ⓑ Ⓒ Ⓓ Ⓔ
17 Ⓐ Ⓑ Ⓒ Ⓓ Ⓔ
18 Ⓐ Ⓑ Ⓒ Ⓓ Ⓔ
19 Ⓐ Ⓑ Ⓒ Ⓓ Ⓔ
20 Ⓐ Ⓑ Ⓒ Ⓓ Ⓔ
21 Ⓐ Ⓑ Ⓒ Ⓓ Ⓔ
22 Ⓐ Ⓑ Ⓒ Ⓓ Ⓔ
23 Ⓐ Ⓑ Ⓒ Ⓓ Ⓔ
24 Ⓐ Ⓑ Ⓒ Ⓓ Ⓔ
25 Ⓐ Ⓑ Ⓒ Ⓓ Ⓔ
26 Ⓐ Ⓑ Ⓒ Ⓓ Ⓔ
27 Ⓐ Ⓑ Ⓒ Ⓓ Ⓔ
28 Ⓐ Ⓑ Ⓒ Ⓓ Ⓔ
29 Ⓐ Ⓑ Ⓒ Ⓓ Ⓔ
30 Ⓐ Ⓑ Ⓒ Ⓓ Ⓔ

SECTION 4

1 Ⓐ Ⓑ Ⓒ Ⓓ Ⓔ
2 Ⓐ Ⓑ Ⓒ Ⓓ Ⓔ
3 Ⓐ Ⓑ Ⓒ Ⓓ Ⓔ
4 Ⓐ Ⓑ Ⓒ Ⓓ Ⓔ
5 Ⓐ Ⓑ Ⓒ Ⓓ Ⓔ
6 Ⓐ Ⓑ Ⓒ Ⓓ Ⓔ
7 Ⓐ Ⓑ Ⓒ Ⓓ Ⓔ
8 Ⓐ Ⓑ Ⓒ Ⓓ Ⓔ
9 Ⓐ Ⓑ Ⓒ Ⓓ Ⓔ
10 Ⓐ Ⓑ Ⓒ Ⓓ Ⓔ
11 Ⓐ Ⓑ Ⓒ Ⓓ Ⓔ
12 Ⓐ Ⓑ Ⓒ Ⓓ Ⓔ
13 Ⓐ Ⓑ Ⓒ Ⓓ Ⓔ
14 Ⓐ Ⓑ Ⓒ Ⓓ Ⓔ
15 Ⓐ Ⓑ Ⓒ Ⓓ Ⓔ
16 Ⓐ Ⓑ Ⓒ Ⓓ Ⓔ
17 Ⓐ Ⓑ Ⓒ Ⓓ Ⓔ
18 Ⓐ Ⓑ Ⓒ Ⓓ Ⓔ
19 Ⓐ Ⓑ Ⓒ Ⓓ Ⓔ
20 Ⓐ Ⓑ Ⓒ Ⓓ Ⓔ
21 Ⓐ Ⓑ Ⓒ Ⓓ Ⓔ
22 Ⓐ Ⓑ Ⓒ Ⓓ Ⓔ
23 Ⓐ Ⓑ Ⓒ Ⓓ Ⓔ
24 Ⓐ Ⓑ Ⓒ Ⓓ Ⓔ
25 Ⓐ Ⓑ Ⓒ Ⓓ Ⓔ
26 Ⓐ Ⓑ Ⓒ Ⓓ Ⓔ
27 Ⓐ Ⓑ Ⓒ Ⓓ Ⓔ
28 Ⓐ Ⓑ Ⓒ Ⓓ Ⓔ
29 Ⓐ Ⓑ Ⓒ Ⓓ Ⓔ
30 Ⓐ Ⓑ Ⓒ Ⓓ Ⓔ

SECTION 5

1 Ⓐ Ⓑ Ⓒ Ⓓ Ⓔ
2 Ⓐ Ⓑ Ⓒ Ⓓ Ⓔ
3 Ⓐ Ⓑ Ⓒ Ⓓ Ⓔ
4 Ⓐ Ⓑ Ⓒ Ⓓ Ⓔ
5 Ⓐ Ⓑ Ⓒ Ⓓ Ⓔ
6 Ⓐ Ⓑ Ⓒ Ⓓ Ⓔ
7 Ⓐ Ⓑ Ⓒ Ⓓ Ⓔ
8 Ⓐ Ⓑ Ⓒ Ⓓ Ⓔ
9 Ⓐ Ⓑ Ⓒ Ⓓ Ⓔ
10 Ⓐ Ⓑ Ⓒ Ⓓ Ⓔ
11 Ⓐ Ⓑ Ⓒ Ⓓ Ⓔ
12 Ⓐ Ⓑ Ⓒ Ⓓ Ⓔ
13 Ⓐ Ⓑ Ⓒ Ⓓ Ⓔ
14 Ⓐ Ⓑ Ⓒ Ⓓ Ⓔ
15 Ⓐ Ⓑ Ⓒ Ⓓ Ⓔ
16 Ⓐ Ⓑ Ⓒ Ⓓ Ⓔ
17 Ⓐ Ⓑ Ⓒ Ⓓ Ⓔ
18 Ⓐ Ⓑ Ⓒ Ⓓ Ⓔ
19 Ⓐ Ⓑ Ⓒ Ⓓ Ⓔ
20 Ⓐ Ⓑ Ⓒ Ⓓ Ⓔ
21 Ⓐ Ⓑ Ⓒ Ⓓ Ⓔ
22 Ⓐ Ⓑ Ⓒ Ⓓ Ⓔ
23 Ⓐ Ⓑ Ⓒ Ⓓ Ⓔ
24 Ⓐ Ⓑ Ⓒ Ⓓ Ⓔ
25 Ⓐ Ⓑ Ⓒ Ⓓ Ⓔ
26 Ⓐ Ⓑ Ⓒ Ⓓ Ⓔ
27 Ⓐ Ⓑ Ⓒ Ⓓ Ⓔ
28 Ⓐ Ⓑ Ⓒ Ⓓ Ⓔ
29 Ⓐ Ⓑ Ⓒ Ⓓ Ⓔ
30 Ⓐ Ⓑ Ⓒ Ⓓ Ⓔ

14 PLEASE PRINT ALL INFORMATION

LAST NAME   FIRST

SOCIAL SECURITY/SOCIAL INSURANCE NO.

DATE OF BIRTH

MAILING ADDRESS

NOTE: If you have a new address you must write LSAC at Box 2000-C, Newtown, PA 18940 or call 215.968.1001.

FOR LSAC USE ONLY

LR	LW	LCS

SECTION I

Time—35 minutes

25 Questions

Directions: The questions in this section are based on the reasoning contained in brief statements or passages. For some questions, more than one of the choices could conceivably answer the question. However, you are to choose the best answer; that is, the response that most accurately and completely answers the question. You should not make assumptions that are by commonsense standards implausible, superfluous, or incompatible with the passage. After you have chosen the best answer, blacken the corresponding space on your answer sheet.

1. The editor of a magazine has pointed out several errors of spelling and grammar committed on a recent TV program. But she can hardly be trusted to pass judgment on such matters: similar errors have been found in her own magazine.

   The flawed reasoning in the argument above is most similar to that in which one of the following?

   (A)   Your newspaper cannot be trusted with the prerogative to criticize the ethics of our company: you misspelled our president's name.
   (B)   Your news program cannot be trusted to judge our hiring practices as unfair: you yourselves unfairly discriminate in hiring and promotion decisions.
   (C)   Your regulatory agency cannot condemn our product as unsafe: selling it is allowed under an existing-product clause.
   (D)   Your coach cannot be trusted to judge our swimming practices: he accepted a lucrative promotional deal from a soft-drink company.
   (E)   Your teen magazine should not run this feature on problems afflicting modern high schools: your revenue depends on not alienating the high school audience.

2. Soaking dried beans overnight before cooking them reduces cooking time. However, cooking without presoaking yields plumper beans. Therefore, when a bean dish's quality is more important than the need to cook that dish quickly, beans should not be presoaked.

   Which one of the following is an assumption required by the argument?

   (A)   Plumper beans enhance the quality of a dish.
   (B)   There are no dishes whose quality improves with faster cooking.
   (C)   A dish's appearance is as important as its taste.
   (D)   None of the other ingredients in the dish need to be presoaked.
   (E)   The plumper the bean, the better it tastes.

3. Durth: Increasingly, businesses use direct mail advertising instead of paying for advertising space in newspapers, in magazines, or on billboards. This practice is annoying and also immoral. Most direct mail advertisements are thrown out without ever being read, and the paper on which they are printed is wasted. If anyone else wasted this much paper, it would be considered unconscionable.

   Which one of the following most accurately describes Durth's method of reasoning?

   (A)   presenting a specific counterexample to the contention that direct mail advertising is not immoral
   (B)   asserting that there would be very undesirable consequences if direct mail advertising became a more widespread practice than it is now
   (C)   claiming that direct mail advertising is immoral because one of its results would be deemed immoral in other contexts
   (D)   basing a conclusion on the claim that direct mail advertising is annoying to those who receive it
   (E)   asserting that other advertising methods do not have the negative effects of direct mail advertising

GO ON TO THE NEXT PAGE.

4. Among the various models of Delta vacuum cleaners, one cannot accurately predict how effectively a particular model cleans simply by determining how powerful its motor is. The efficiency of dust filtration systems varies significantly, even between models of Delta vacuum cleaners equipped with identically powerful motors.

The argument's conclusion is properly drawn if which one of the following is assumed?

(A) For each Delta vacuum cleaner, the efficiency of its dust filtration system has a significant impact on how effectively it cleans.

(B) One can accurately infer how powerful a Delta vacuum cleaner's motor is from the efficiency of the vacuum cleaner's dust filtration system.

(C) All Delta vacuum cleaners that clean equally effectively have identically powerful motors.

(D) For any two Delta vacuum cleaners with equally efficient dust filtration systems, the one with the more powerful motor cleans more effectively.

(E) One cannot accurately assess how effectively any Delta vacuum cleaner cleans without knowing how powerful that vacuum cleaner's motor is.

5. Many scientists believe that bipedal locomotion (walking on two feet) evolved in early hominids in response to the move from life in dense forests to life in open grasslands. Bipedalism would have allowed early hominids to see over tall grasses, helping them to locate food and to detect and avoid predators. However, because bipedalism also would have conferred substantial advantages upon early hominids who never left the forest—in gathering food found within standing reach of the forest floor, for example—debate continues concerning its origins. It may even have evolved, like the upright threat displays of many large apes, because it bettered an individual's odds of finding a mate.

Which one of the following statements is most supported by the information above?

(A) For early hominids, forest environments were generally more hospitable than grassland environments.

(B) Bipedal locomotion would have helped early hominids gather food.

(C) Bipedal locomotion actually would not be advantageous to hominids living in open grassland environments.

(D) Bipedal locomotion probably evolved among early hominids who exclusively inhabited forest environments.

(E) For early hominids, gathering food was more relevant to survival than was detecting and avoiding predators.

6. Mathematics teacher: Teaching students calculus before they attend university may significantly benefit them. Yet if students are taught calculus before they are ready for the level of abstraction involved, they may abandon the study of mathematics altogether. So if we are going to teach pre-university students calculus, we must make sure they can handle the level of abstraction involved.

Which one of the following principles most helps to justify the mathematics teacher's argument?

(A) Only those who, without losing motivation, can meet the cognitive challenges that new intellectual work involves should be introduced to it.

(B) Only those parts of university-level mathematics that are the most concrete should be taught to pre-university students.

(C) Cognitive tasks that require exceptional effort tend to undermine the motivation of those who attempt them.

(D) Teachers who teach university-level mathematics to pre-university students should be aware that students are likely to learn effectively only when the application of mathematics to concrete problems is shown.

(E) The level of abstraction involved in a topic should not be considered in determining whether that topic is appropriate for pre-university students.

GO ON TO THE NEXT PAGE.

7. In 1955, legislation in a certain country gave the government increased control over industrial workplace safety conditions. Among the high-risk industries in that country, the likelihood that a worker will suffer a serious injury has decreased since 1955. The legislation, therefore, has increased overall worker safety within high-risk industries.

Which one of the following, if true, most weakens the argument above?

(A) Because of technological innovation, most workplaces in the high-risk industries do not require as much unprotected interaction between workers and heavy machinery as they did in 1955.

(B) Most of the work-related injuries that occurred before 1955 were the result of worker carelessness.

(C) The annual number of work-related injuries has increased since the legislation took effect.

(D) The number of work-related injuries occurring within industries not considered high-risk has increased annually since 1955.

(E) Workplace safety conditions in all industries have improved steadily since 1955.

8. Economist: Historically, sunflower seed was one of the largest production crops in Kalotopia, and it continues to be a major source of income for several countries. The renewed growing of sunflowers would provide relief to Kalotopia's farming industry, which is quite unstable. Further, sunflower oil can provide a variety of products, both industrial and consumer, at little cost to Kalotopia's already fragile environment.

The economist's statements, if true, most strongly support which one of the following?

(A) Kalotopia's farming industry will deteriorate if sunflowers are not grown there.

(B) Stabilizing Kalotopia's farming industry would improve the economy without damaging the environment.

(C) Kalotopia's farming industry would be better off now if it had never ceased to grow any of the crops that historically were large production crops.

(D) A crop that was once a large production crop in Kalotopia would, if it were grown there again, benefit that country's farmers and general economy.

(E) Sunflower seed is a better crop for Kalotopia from both the environmental and the economic viewpoints than are most crops that could be grown there.

9. Several major earthquakes have occurred in a certain region over the last ten years. But a new earthquake prediction method promises to aid local civil defense officials in deciding exactly when to evacuate various towns. Detected before each of these major quakes were certain changes in the electric current in the earth's crust.

Which one of the following, if true, most weakens the argument?

(A) Scientists do not fully understand what brought about the changes in the electric current in the earth's crust that preceded each of the major quakes in the region over the last ten years.

(B) Most other earthquake prediction methods have been based on a weaker correlation than that found between the changes in the electric current in the earth's crust and the subsequent earthquakes.

(C) The frequency of major earthquakes in the region has increased over the last ten years.

(D) There is considerable variation in the length of time between the changes in the electric current and the subsequent earthquakes.

(E) There is presently only one station in the region that is capable of detecting the electric current in the earth's crust.

10. Unlike many machines that are perfectly useful in isolation from others, fax machines must work with other fax machines. Thus, in the fax industry, the proliferation of incompatible formats, which resulted from the large number of competing manufacturers, severely limited the usefulness—and hence the commercial viability—of fax technology until the manufacturers agreed to adopt a common format for their machines.

The information above provides the most support for which one of the following propositions?

(A) Whenever machines are dependent on other machines of the same type, competition among manufacturers is damaging to the industry.

(B) In some industries it is in the interest of competitors to cooperate to some extent with one another.

(C) The more competitors there are in a high-tech industry, the more they will have to cooperate in determining the basic design of their product.

(D) Some cooperation among manufacturers in the same industry is more beneficial than is pure competition.

(E) Cooperation is beneficial only in industries whose products depend on other products of the same type.

GO ON TO THE NEXT PAGE.

11. In comparing different methods by which a teacher's performance can be evaluated and educational outcomes improved, researchers found that a critique of teacher performance leads to enhanced educational outcomes if the critique is accompanied by the information that teacher performance is merely one of several factors that, in concert with other factors, determines the educational outcomes.

Which one of the following best illustrates the principle illustrated by the finding of the researchers?

(A) Children can usually be taught to master subject matter in which they have no interest if they believe that successfully mastering it will earn the respect of their peers.

(B) People are generally more willing to accept a negative characterization of a small group of people if they do not see themselves as members of the group being so characterized.

(C) An actor can more effectively evaluate the merits of her own performance if she can successfully convince herself that she is really evaluating the performance of another actor.

(D) The opinions reached by a social scientist in the study of a society can be considered as more reliable and objective if that social scientist is not a member of that society.

(E) It is easier to correct the mistakes of an athlete if it is made clear to him that the criticism is part of an overarching effort to rectify the shortcomings of the entire team on which he plays.

12. Critic: A novel cannot be of the highest quality unless most readers become emotionally engaged with the imaginary world it describes. Thus shifts of narrative point of view within a novel, either between first and third person or of some other sort, detract from the merit of the work, since such shifts tend to make most readers focus on the author.

Which one of the following is an assumption necessary for the critic's conclusion to be properly drawn?

(A) Most readers become emotionally engaged with the imaginary world described by a novel only if the novel is of the highest quality.

(B) A novel is generally not considered to be of high quality unless it successfully engages the imagination of most readers.

(C) Most readers cannot become emotionally involved with a novel's imaginary world if they focus on the author.

(D) Most readers regard a novel's narrative point of view as representing the perspective of the novel's author.

(E) Shifts in narrative point of view serve no literary purpose.

13. People aged 46 to 55 spend more money per capita than people of any other age group. So it is puzzling that when companies advertise consumer products on television, they focus almost exclusively on people aged 25 and under. Indeed, those who make decisions about television advertising think that the value of a television advertising slot depends entirely on the number of people aged 25 and under who can be expected to be watching at that time.

Which one of the following, if true, most helps to explain the puzzling facts stated above?

(A) The expense of television advertising slots makes it crucial for companies to target people who are most likely to purchase their products.

(B) Advertising slots during news programs almost always cost far less than advertising slots during popular sitcoms whose leading characters are young adults.

(C) When television executives decide which shows to renew, they do so primarily in terms of the shows' ratings among people aged 25 and under.

(D) Those who make decisions about television advertising believe that people older than 25 almost never change their buying habits.

(E) When companies advertise consumer products in print media, they focus primarily on people aged 26 and over.

14. Eighteenth-century moralist: You should never make an effort to acquire expensive new tastes, since they are a drain on your purse and in the course of acquiring them you may expose yourself to sensations that are obnoxious to you. Furthermore, the very effort that must be expended in their acquisition attests their superfluity.

The moralist's reasoning is most vulnerable to criticism on the grounds that the moralist

(A) draws a conclusion that simply restates a claim presented in support of that conclusion

(B) takes for granted that the acquisition of expensive tastes will lead to financial irresponsibility

(C) uses the inherently vague term "sensations" without providing a definition of that term

(D) mistakes a cause of acquisition of expensive tastes for an effect of acquisition of such tastes

(E) rejects trying to achieve a goal because of the cost of achieving it, without considering the benefits of achieving it

GO ON TO THE NEXT PAGE.

15. Zack's Coffeehouse schedules free poetry readings almost every Wednesday. Zack's offers half-priced coffee all day on every day that a poetry reading is scheduled.

Which one of the following can be properly inferred from the information above?

(A) Wednesday is the most common day on which Zack's offers half-priced coffee all day.

(B) Most free poetry readings given at Zack's are scheduled for Wednesdays.

(C) Free poetry readings are scheduled on almost every day that Zack's offers half-priced coffee all day.

(D) Zack's offers half-priced coffee all day on most if not all Wednesdays.

(E) On some Wednesdays Zack's does not offer half-priced coffee all day.

16. Philosopher: An event is intentional if it is a human action performed on the basis of a specific motivation. An event is random if it is not performed on the basis of a specific motivation and it is not explainable by normal physical processes.

Which one of the following inferences conforms most closely to the philosopher's position?

(A) Tarik left the keys untouched on the kitchen counter, but he did not do so on the basis of a specific motivation. Therefore, the keys' remaining on the kitchen counter was a random event.

(B) Ellis tore the envelope open in order to read its contents, but the envelope was empty. Nevertheless, because Ellis acted on the basis of a specific motivation, tearing the envelope open was an intentional event.

(C) Judith's hailing a cab distracted a driver in the left lane. She performed the action of hailing the cab on the basis of a specific motivation, so the driver's becoming distracted was an intentional event.

(D) Yasuko continued to breathe regularly throughout the time that she was asleep. This was a human action, but it was not performed on the basis of a specific motivation. Therefore, her breathing was a random event.

(E) Henry lost his hold on the wrench and dropped it because the handle was slippery. This was a human action and is explainable by normal physical processes, so it was an intentional event.

17. It is a mistake to conclude, as some have, that ancient people did not know what moral rights were simply because no known ancient language has an expression correctly translatable as "a moral right." This would be like saying that a person who discovers a wild fruit tree and returns repeatedly to harvest from it and study it has no idea what the fruit is until naming it or learning its name.

Which one of the following is an assumption required by the argument?

(A) To know the name of something is to know what that thing is.

(B) People who first discover what something is know it better than do people who merely know the name of the thing.

(C) The name or expression that is used to identify something cannot provide any information about the nature of the thing that is identified.

(D) A person who repeatedly harvests from a wild fruit tree and studies it has some idea of what the fruit is even before knowing a name for the fruit.

(E) One need not know what something is before one can name it.

18. There is little plausibility to the claim that it is absurd to criticize anyone for being critical. Obviously, people must assess one another and not all assessments will be positive. However, there is wisdom behind the injunction against being judgmental. To be judgmental is not merely to assess someone negatively, but to do so prior to a serious effort at understanding.

Which one of the following most accurately expresses the main conclusion drawn in the argument?

(A) To be judgmental is to assess someone negatively prior to making a serious effort at understanding.

(B) It is absurd to criticize anyone for being critical.

(C) There is some plausibility to the claim that it is absurd to criticize anyone for being critical.

(D) Not all assessments people make of one another will be positive.

(E) There is wisdom behind the injunction against being judgmental.

GO ON TO THE NEXT PAGE.

19. Even those who believe that the art of each age and culture has its own standards of beauty must admit that some painters are simply superior to others in the execution of their artistic visions. But this superiority must be measured in light of the artist's purposes, since the high merits, for example, of Jose Rey Toledo's work and his extraordinary artistic skills are not in doubt, despite the fact that his paintings do not literally resemble what they represent.

The claim that some painters are superior to others in the execution of their artistic visions plays which one of the following roles in the argument?

(A) It is a hypothesis that the argument attempts to refute.

(B) It is a generalization, one sort of objection to which the argument illustrates by giving an example.

(C) It is a claim that, according to the argument, is to be understood in a manner specified by the conclusion.

(D) It is a claim that the argument derives from another claim and that it uses to support its conclusion.

(E) It is a generalization that the argument uses to justify the relevance of the specific example it cites.

20. A study of rabbits in the 1940s convinced many biologists that parthenogenesis—reproduction without fertilization of an egg—sometimes occurs in mammals. However, the study's methods have since been shown to be flawed, and no other studies have succeeded in demonstrating mammalian parthenogenesis. Thus, since parthenogenesis is known to occur in a wide variety of nonmammalian vertebrates, there must be something about mammalian chromosomes that precludes the possibility of parthenogenesis.

A flaw in the reasoning of the argument is that the argument

(A) takes for granted that something that has not been proven to be true is for that reason shown to be false

(B) infers that a characteristic is shared by all nonmammalian vertebrate species merely because it is shared by some nonmammalian vertebrate species

(C) rules out an explanation of a phenomenon merely on the grounds that there is another explanation that can account for the phenomenon

(D) confuses a necessary condition for parthenogenesis with a sufficient condition for it

(E) assumes that the methods used in a study of one mammalian species were flawed merely because the study's findings cannot be generalized to all other mammalian species

21. Advertiser: Most TV shows depend on funding from advertisers and would be canceled without such funding. However, advertisers will not pay to have their commercials aired during a TV show unless many people watching the show buy the advertised products as a result. So if people generally fail to buy the products advertised during their favorite shows, these shows will soon be canceled. Thus, anyone who feels that a TV show is worth preserving ought to buy the products advertised during that show.

The advertiser's reasoning most closely conforms to which one of the following principles?

(A) If a TV show that one feels to be worth preserving would be canceled unless one took certain actions, then one ought to take those actions.

(B) If a TV show would be canceled unless many people took certain actions, then everyone who feels that the show is worth preserving ought to take those actions.

(C) If a TV show is worth preserving, then everyone should take whatever actions are necessary to prevent that show from being canceled.

(D) If one feels that a TV show is worth preserving, then one should take at least some actions to reduce the likelihood that the show will be canceled.

(E) If a TV show would be canceled unless many people took certain actions, then those who feel most strongly that it is worth preserving should take those actions.

GO ON TO THE NEXT PAGE.

22. Psychologist: It is well known that becoming angry often induces temporary incidents of high blood pressure. A recent study further showed, however, that people who are easily angered are significantly more likely to have permanently high blood pressure than are people who have more tranquil personalities. Coupled with the long-established fact that those with permanently high blood pressure are especially likely to have heart disease, the recent findings indicate that heart disease can result from psychological factors.

Which one of the following would, if true, most weaken the psychologist's argument?

(A) Those who are easily angered are less likely to recover fully from episodes of heart disease than are other people.

(B) Medication designed to control high blood pressure can greatly affect the moods of those who use it.

(C) People with permanently high blood pressure who have tranquil personalities virtually never develop heart disease.

(D) Those who discover that they have heart disease tend to become more easily frustrated by small difficulties.

(E) The physiological factors that cause permanently high blood pressure generally make people quick to anger.

23. A professor of business placed a case-study assignment for her class on her university's computer network. She later found out that instead of reading the assignment on the computer screen, 50 out of the 70 students printed it out on paper. Thus, it is not the case that books delivered via computer will make printed books obsolete.

Which one of the following, if true, most strengthens the argument?

(A) Several colleagues of the professor have found that, in their non-business courses, several of their students behave similarly in relation to assignments placed on the computer network.

(B) Studies consistently show that most computer users will print reading material that is more than a few pages in length rather than read it on the computer screen.

(C) Some people get impaired vision from long periods of reading printed matter on computer screens, even if they use high quality computer screens.

(D) Scanning technology is very poor, causing books delivered via computer to be full of errors unless editors carefully read the scanned versions.

(E) Books on cassette tape have only a small fraction of the sales of printed versions of the same books, though sales of videos of books that have been turned into movies remain strong.

GO ON TO THE NEXT PAGE.

24. Advertisement: Researchers studied a group of people trying to lose weight and discovered that those in the group who lost the most weight got more calories from protein than from carbohydrates and ate their biggest meal early in the day. So anyone who follows our diet, which provides more calories from protein than from anything else and which requires that breakfast be the biggest meal of the day, is sure to lose weight.

The reasoning in the advertisement is most vulnerable to criticism on the grounds that the advertisement overlooks the possibility that

(A) eating foods that derive a majority of their calories from carbohydrates tends to make one feel fuller than does eating foods that derive a majority of their calories from protein

(B) a few of the people in the group studied who lost significant amounts of weight got nearly all of their calories from carbohydrates and ate their biggest meal at night

(C) the people in the group studied who increased their activity levels lost more weight, on average, than those who did not, regardless of whether they got more calories from protein or from carbohydrates

(D) some people in the group studied lost no weight yet got more calories from protein than from carbohydrates and ate their biggest meal early in the day

(E) people who eat their biggest meal at night tend to snack more during the day and so tend to take in more total calories than do people who eat their biggest meal earlier in the day

25. Some twentieth-century art is great art. All great art involves original ideas, and any art that is not influential cannot be great art.

Each of the following statements follows logically from the set of statements above EXCEPT:

(A) Some influential art involves original ideas.
(B) Some twentieth-century art involves original ideas.
(C) Only art that involves original ideas is influential.
(D) Only art that is influential and involves original ideas is great art.
(E) Some twentieth-century art is influential and involves original ideas.

S T O P
IF YOU FINISH BEFORE TIME IS CALLED, YOU MAY CHECK YOUR WORK ON THIS SECTION ONLY.
DO NOT WORK ON ANY OTHER SECTION IN THE TEST.

SECTION II

Time—35 minutes

27 Questions

Directions: Each set of questions in this section is based on a single passage or a pair of passages. The questions are to be answered on the basis of what is <u>stated</u> or <u>implied</u> in the passage or pair of passages. For some of the questions, more than one of the choices could conceivably answer the question. However, you are to choose the <u>best</u> answer; that is, the response that most accurately and completely answers the question, and blacken the corresponding space on your answer sheet.

Often when a highly skilled and experienced employee leaves one company to work for another, there is the potential for a transfer of sensitive information between competitors. Two basic principles
(5) in such cases appear irreconcilable: the right of the company to its intellectual property—its proprietary data and trade secrets—and the right of individuals to seek gainful employment and to make free use of their abilities. Nevertheless, the courts have often tried to
(10) preserve both parties' legal rights by refusing to prohibit the employee from working for the competitor, but at the same time providing an injunction against disclosure of any of the former employer's secrets. It has been argued that because such measures help
(15) generate suspicions and similar psychological barriers to full and free utilization of abilities in the employee's new situation, they are hardly effective in upholding the individual's rights to free employment decisions. But it is also doubtful that they are effective in
(20) preserving trade secrets.

It is obviously impossible to divest oneself of that part of one's expertise that one has acquired from former employers and coworkers. Nor, in general, can one selectively refrain from its use, given that it has
(25) become an integral part of one's total intellectual capacity. Nevertheless, almost any such information that is not public knowledge may legitimately be claimed as corporate property: normal employment agreements provide for corporate ownership of all
(30) relevant data, including inventions, generated by the employee in connection with the company's business.

Once an employee takes a position with a competitor, the trade secrets that have been acquired by that employee may manifest themselves clearly and
(35) consciously. This is what court injunctions seek to prohibit. But they are far more likely to manifest themselves subconsciously and inconspicuously—for example, in one's daily decisions at the new post, or in the many small contributions one might make to a large
(40) team effort—often in the form of an intuitive sense of what to do or to avoid. Theoretically, an injunction also prohibits such inadvertent "leakage." However, the former employer faces the practical problem of securing evidence of such leakage, for little will
(45) usually be apparent from the public activities of the new employer. And even if the new employee's activities appear suspicious, there is the further problem of distinguishing trade secrets from what may be legitimately asserted as technological skills
(50) developed independently by the employee or already possessed by the new employer. This is a major stumbling block in the attempt to protect trade secrets,

since the proprietor has no recourse against others who independently generate the same information. It is
(55) therefore unlikely that an injunction against disclosure of trade secrets to future employers actually prevents any transfer of information except for the passage of documents and other concrete embodiments of the secrets.

1. Which one of the following most accurately expresses the main point of the passage?

(A) There are more effective ways than court injunctions to preserve both a company's right to protect its intellectual property and individuals' rights to make free use of their abilities.

(B) Court injunctions must be strengthened if they are to remain a relevant means of protecting corporations' trade secrets.

(C) Enforcement of court injunctions designed to protect proprietary information is impossible when employees reveal such information to new employers.

(D) Court injunctions prohibiting employees from disclosing former employers' trade secrets to new employers probably do not achieve all of their intended objectives.

(E) The rights of employees to make full use of their talents and previous training are being seriously eroded by the prohibitions placed on them by court injunctions designed to prevent the transfer of trade secrets.

GO ON TO THE NEXT PAGE.

2. Given the passage's content and tone, which one of the following statements would most likely be found elsewhere in a work from which this passage is an excerpt?

(A) Given the law as it stands, corporations concerned about preserving trade secrets might be best served by giving their employees strong incentives to stay in their current jobs.

(B) While difficult to enforce and interpret, injunctions are probably the most effective means of halting the inadvertent transfer of trade secrets while simultaneously protecting the rights of employees.

(C) Means of redress must be made available to companies that suspect, but cannot prove, that former employees are revealing protected information to competitors.

(D) Even concrete materials such as computer disks are so easy to copy and conceal that it will be a waste of time for courts to try to prevent the spread of information through physical theft.

(E) The psychological barriers that an injunction can place on an employee in a new workplace are inevitably so subtle that they have no effect on the employee.

3. The author's primary purpose in the passage is to

(A) suggest that injunctions against the disclosure of trade secrets not only create problems for employees in the workplace, but also are unable to halt the illicit spread of proprietary information

(B) suggest that the information contained in "documents and other concrete embodiments" is usually so trivial that injunctions do little good in protecting intellectual property

(C) argue that new methods must be found to address the delicate balance between corporate and individual rights

(D) support the position that the concept of protecting trade secrets is no longer viable in an age of increasing access to information

(E) argue that injunctions are not necessary for the protection of trade secrets

4. The passage provides the most support for which one of the following assertions?

(A) Injunctions should be imposed by the courts only when there is strong reason to believe that an employee will reveal proprietary information.

(B) There is apparently no reliable way to protect both the rights of companies to protect trade secrets and the rights of employees to seek new employment.

(C) Employees should not be allowed to take jobs with their former employers' competitors when their new job could compromise trade secrets of their former employers.

(D) The multiplicity of means for transferring information in the workplace only increases the need for injunctions.

(E) Some companies seek injunctions as a means of punishing employees who take jobs with their competitors.

5. With which one of the following statements regarding documents and other concrete embodiments mentioned in line 58 would the author be most likely to agree?

(A) While the transfer of such materials would be damaging, even the seemingly innocuous contributions of an employee to a competitor can do more harm in the long run.

(B) Such materials are usually less informative than what the employee may recollect about a previous job.

(C) Injunctions against the disclosure of trade secrets should carefully specify which materials are included in order to focus on the most damaging ones.

(D) Large-scale transfer of documents and other materials cannot be controlled by injunctions.

(E) Such concrete materials lend themselves to control and identification more readily than do subtler means of transferring information.

6. In the passage, the author makes which one of the following claims?

(A) Injunctions against the disclosure of trade secrets limit an employee's chances of being hired by a competitor.

(B) Measures against the disclosure of trade secrets are unnecessary except in the case of documents and other concrete embodiments of the secrets.

(C) Employees who switch jobs to work for a competitor usually unintentionally violate the law by doing so.

(D) Employers are not restricted in the tactics they can use when seeking to secure protected information from new employees.

(E) What may seem like intellectual theft may in fact be an example of independent innovation.

GO ON TO THE NEXT PAGE.

The following passages concern a plant called purple loosestrife. Passage A is excerpted from a report issued by a prairie research council; passage B from a journal of sociology.

Passage A

Purple loosestrife (*Lythrum salicaria*), an aggressive and invasive perennial of Eurasian origin, arrived with settlers in eastern North America in the early 1800s and has spread across the continent's
(5) midlatitude wetlands. The impact of purple loosestrife on native vegetation has been disastrous, with more than 50 percent of the biomass of some wetland communities displaced. Monospecific blocks of this weed have maintained themselves for at least 20 years.
(10) Impacts on wildlife have not been well studied, but serious reductions in waterfowl and aquatic furbearer productivity have been observed. In addition, several endangered species of vertebrates are threatened with further degradation of their
(15) breeding habitats. Although purple loosestrife can invade relatively undisturbed habitats, the spread and dominance of this weed have been greatly accelerated in disturbed habitats. While digging out the plants can temporarily halt their spread, there has been little
(20) research on long-term purple loosestrife control. Glyphosate has been used successfully, but no measure of the impact of this herbicide on native plant communities has been made.

With the spread of purple loosestrife growing
(25) exponentially, some form of integrated control is needed. At present, coping with purple loosestrife hinges on early detection of the weed's arrival in areas, which allows local eradication to be carried out with minimum damage to the native plant community.

Passage B

(30) The war on purple loosestrife is apparently conducted on behalf of nature, an attempt to liberate the biotic community from the tyrannical influence of a life-destroying invasive weed. Indeed, purple loosestrife control is portrayed by its practitioners as
(35) an environmental initiative intended to save nature rather than control it. Accordingly, the purple loosestrife literature, scientific and otherwise, dutifully discusses the impacts of the weed on endangered species—and on threatened biodiversity
(40) more generally. Purple loosestrife is a pollution, according to the scientific community, and all of nature suffers under its pervasive influence.

Regardless of the perceived and actual ecological effects of the purple invader, it is apparent that
(45) popular pollution ideologies have been extended into the wetlands of North America. Consequently, the scientific effort to liberate nature from purple loosestrife has failed to decouple itself from its philosophical origin as an instrument to control nature
(50) to the satisfaction of human desires. Birds, particularly game birds and waterfowl, provide the bulk of the justification for loosestrife management. However, no bird species other than the canvasback has been identified in the literature as endangered by

(55) purple loosestrife. The impact of purple loosestrife on furbearing mammals is discussed at great length, though none of the species highlighted (muskrat, mink) can be considered threatened in North America. What is threatened by purple loosestrife is the
(60) economics of exploiting such preferred species and the millions of dollars that will be lost to the economies of the United States and Canada from reduced hunting, trapping, and recreation revenues due to a decline in the production of the wetland
(65) resource.

7. Both passages explicitly mention which one of the following?

(A) furbearing animals
(B) glyphosate
(C) the threat purple loosestrife poses to economies
(D) popular pollution ideologies
(E) literature on purple loosestrife control

8. Each of the passages contains information sufficient to answer which one of the following questions?

(A) Approximately how long ago did purple loosestrife arrive in North America?
(B) Is there much literature discussing the potential benefit that hunters might derive from purple loosestrife management?
(C) What is an issue regarding purple loosestrife management on which both hunters and farmers agree?
(D) Is the canvasback threatened with extinction due to the spread of purple loosestrife?
(E) What is a type of terrain that is affected in at least some parts of North America by the presence of purple loosestrife?

9. It can be inferred that the authors would be most likely to disagree about which one of the following?

(A) Purple loosestrife spreads more quickly in disturbed habitats than in undisturbed habitats.
(B) The threat posed by purple loosestrife to local aquatic furbearer populations is serious.
(C) Most people who advocate that eradication measures be taken to control purple loosestrife are not genuine in their concern for the environment.
(D) The size of the biomass that has been displaced by purple loosestrife is larger than is generally thought.
(E) Measures should be taken to prevent other non-native plant species from invading North America.

GO ON TO THE NEXT PAGE.

10. Which one of the following most accurately describes the attitude expressed by the author of passage B toward the overall argument represented by passage A?

(A) enthusiastic agreement
(B) cautious agreement
(C) pure neutrality
(D) general ambivalence
(E) pointed skepticism

11. It can be inferred that both authors would be most likely to agree with which one of the following statements regarding purple loosestrife?

(A) As it increases in North America, some wildlife populations tend to decrease.
(B) Its establishment in North America has had a disastrous effect on native North American wetland vegetation in certain regions.
(C) It is very difficult to control effectively with herbicides.
(D) Its introduction into North America was a great ecological blunder.
(E) When it is eliminated from a given area, it tends to return to that area fairly quickly.

12. Which one of the following is true about the relationship between the two passages?

(A) Passage A presents evidence that directly counters claims made in passage B.
(B) Passage B assumes what passage A explicitly argues for.
(C) Passage B displays an awareness of the arguments touched on in passage A, but not vice versa.
(D) Passage B advocates a policy that passage A rejects.
(E) Passage A downplays the seriousness of claims made in passage B.

13. Which one of the following, if true, would cast doubt on the argument in passage B but bolster the argument in passage A?

(A) Localized population reduction is often a precursor to widespread endangerment of a species.
(B) Purple loosestrife was barely noticed in North America before the advent of suburban sprawl in the 1950s.
(C) The amount by which overall hunting, trapping, and recreation revenues would be reduced as a result of the extinction of one or more species threatened by purple loosestrife represents a significant portion of those revenues.
(D) Some environmentalists who advocate taking measures to eradicate purple loosestrife view such measures as a means of controlling nature.
(E) Purple loosestrife has never become a problem in its native habitat, even though no effort has been made to eradicate it there.

GO ON TO THE NEXT PAGE.

With their recognition of Maxine Hong Kingston as a major literary figure, some critics have suggested that her works have been produced almost *ex nihilo*, saying that they lack a large traceable body of direct
(5) literary antecedents especially within the Chinese American heritage in which her work is embedded. But these critics, who have examined only the development of written texts, the most visible signs of a culture's narrative production, have overlooked Kingston's
(10) connection to the long Chinese tradition of a highly developed genre of song and spoken narrative known as "talk-story" (*gong gu tsai*).

Traditionally performed in the dialects of various ethnic enclaves, talk-story has been maintained within
(15) the confines of the family and has rarely surfaced into print. The tradition dates back to Sung dynasty (A.D. 970–1279) storytellers in China, and in the United States it is continually revitalized by an overlapping sequence of immigration from China.
(20) Thus, Chinese immigrants to the U.S. had a fully established, sophisticated oral culture, already ancient and capable of producing masterpieces, by the time they began arriving in the early nineteenth century. This transplanted oral heritage simply embraced new
(25) subject matter or new forms of Western discourse, as in the case of Kingston's adaptations written in English.

Kingston herself believes that as a literary artist she is one in a long line of performers shaping a recalcitrant history into talk-story form. She
(30) distinguishes her "thematic" storytelling memory processes, which sift and reconstruct the essential elements of personally remembered stories, from the memory processes of a print-oriented culture that emphasizes the retention of precise sequences of
(35) words. Nor does the entry of print into the storytelling process substantially change her notion of the character of oral tradition. For Kingston, "writer" is synonymous with "singer" or "performer" in the ancient sense of privileged keeper, transmitter, and creator of stories
(40) whose current stage of development can be frozen in print, but which continue to grow both around and from that frozen text.

Kingston's participation in the tradition of talk-story is evidenced in her book *China Men*, which
(45) utilizes forms typical of that genre and common to most oral cultures including: a fixed "grammar" of repetitive themes; a spectrum of stock characters; symmetrical structures, including balanced oppositions (verbal or physical contests, antithetical characters,
(50) dialectical discourse such as question-answer forms and riddles); and repetition. In *China Men*, Kingston also succeeds in investing idiomatic English with the allusive texture and oral-aural qualities of the Chinese language, a language rich in aural and visual puns,
(55) making her work a written form of talk-story.

14. Which one of the following most accurately states the main point of the passage?

(A) Despite some critics' comments, Kingston's writings have significant Chinese American antecedents, which can be found in the traditional oral narrative form known as talk-story.

(B) Analysis of Kingston's writings, especially *China Men*, supports her belief that literary artists can be performers who continue to reconstruct their stories even after they have been frozen in print.

(C) An understanding of Kingston's work and of Chinese American writers in general reveals that critics of ethnic literatures in the United States have been mistaken in examining only written texts.

(D) Throughout her writings Kingston uses techniques typical of the talk-story genre, especially the retention of certain aspects of Chinese speech in the written English text.

(E) The writings of Kingston have rekindled an interest in talk-story, which dates back to the Sung dynasty, and was extended to the United States with the arrival of Chinese immigrants in the nineteenth century.

15. Which one of the following can be most reasonably inferred from the passage?

(A) In the last few years, written forms of talk-story have appeared in Chinese as often as they have in English.

(B) Until very recently, scholars have held that oral storytelling in Chinese ethnic enclaves was a unique oral tradition.

(C) Talk-story has developed in the United States through a process of combining Chinese, Chinese American, and other oral storytelling forms.

(D) Chinese American talk-story relies upon memory processes that do not emphasize the retention of precise sequences of words.

(E) The connection between certain aspects of Kingston's work and talk-story is argued by some critics to be rather tenuous and questionable.

GO ON TO THE NEXT PAGE.

16. It can be inferred from the passage that the author uses the phrase "personally remembered stories" (line 32) primarily to refer to

(A) a literary genre of first-person storytelling
(B) a thematically organized personal narrative of one's own past
(C) partially idiosyncratic memories of narratives
(D) the retention in memory of precise sequences of words
(E) easily identifiable thematic issues in literature

17. In which one of the following is the use of cotton fibers or cotton cloth most analogous to Kingston's use of the English language as described in lines 51–55?

(A) Scraps of plain cotton cloth are used to create a multicolored quilt.
(B) The surface texture of woolen cloth is simulated in a piece of cotton cloth by a special process of weaving.
(C) Because of its texture, cotton cloth is used for a certain type of clothes for which linen is inappropriate.
(D) In making a piece of cloth, cotton fiber is substituted for linen because of the roughly similar texture of the two materials.
(E) Because of their somewhat similar textures, cotton and linen fibers are woven together in a piece of cloth to achieve a savings in price over a pure linen cloth.

18. The passage most clearly suggests that Kingston believes which one of the following about at least some of the stories contained in her writings?

(A) Since they are intimately tied to the nature of the Chinese language, they can be approximated, but not adequately expressed, in English.
(B) They should be thought of primarily as ethnic literature and evaluated accordingly by critics.
(C) They will likely be retold and altered to some extent in the process.
(D) Chinese American history is best chronicled by traditional talk-story.
(E) Their significance and beauty cannot be captured at all in written texts.

19. The author's argument in the passage would be most weakened if which one of the following were true?

(A) Numerous writers in the United States have been influenced by oral traditions.
(B) Most Chinese American writers' work is very different from Kingston's.
(C) Native American storytellers use narrative devices similar to those used in talk-story.
(D) *China Men* is for the most part atypical of Kingston's literary works.
(E) Literary critics generally appreciate the authenticity of Kingston's work.

20. The author's specific purpose in detailing typical talk-story forms (lines 43–51) is to

(A) show why Kingston's book *China Men* establishes her as a major literary figure
(B) support the claim that Kingston's use of typically oral techniques makes her work a part of the talk-story tradition
(C) dispute the critics' view that Chinese American literature lacks literary antecedents
(D) argue for Kingston's view that the literary artist is at best a "privileged keeper" of stories
(E) provide an alternative to certain critics' view that Kingston's work should be judged primarily as literature

21. Which one of the following most accurately identifies the attitude shown by the author in the passage toward talk-story?

(A) scholarly appreciation for its longstanding artistic sophistication
(B) mild disappointment that it has not distinguished itself from other oral traditions
(C) tentative approval of its resistance to critical evaluations
(D) clear respect for the diversity of its ancient sources and cultural derivations
(E) open admiration for the way it uses song to express narrative

GO ON TO THE NEXT PAGE.

In economics, the term "speculative bubble"
refers to a large upward move in an asset's price
driven not by the asset's fundamentals—that is, by
the earnings derivable from the asset—but rather by
(5)   mere speculation that someone else will be willing to
pay a higher price for it. The price increase is then
followed by a dramatic decline in price, due to a loss
in confidence that the price will continue to rise, and
the "bubble" is said to have burst. According to
(10) Charles Mackay's classic nineteenth-century account,
the seventeenth-century Dutch tulip market provides
an example of a speculative bubble. But the
economist Peter Garber challenges Mackay's view,
arguing that there is no evidence that the Dutch tulip
(15) market really involved a speculative bubble.

By the seventeenth century, the Netherlands had
become a center of cultivation and development of
new tulip varieties, and a market had developed in
which rare varieties of bulbs sold at high prices. For
(20) example, a Semper Augustus bulb sold in 1625 for an
amount of gold worth about U.S.$11,000 in 1999.
Common bulb varieties, on the other hand, sold for
very low prices. According to Mackay, by 1636 rapid
price rises attracted speculators, and prices of many
(25) varieties surged upward from November 1636 through
January 1637. Mackay further states that in February
1637 prices suddenly collapsed; bulbs could not be
sold at 10 percent of their peak values. By 1739, the
prices of all the most prized kinds of bulbs had fallen
(30) to no more than one two-hundredth of 1 percent of
Semper Augustus's peak price.

Garber acknowledges that bulb prices increased
dramatically from 1636 to 1637 and eventually
reached very low levels. But he argues that this
(35) episode should not be described as a speculative
bubble, for the increase and eventual decline in bulb
prices can be explained in terms of the fundamentals.
Garber argues that a standard pricing pattern occurs
for new varieties of flowers. When a particularly
(40) prized variety is developed, its original bulb sells for
a high price. Thus, the dramatic rise in the price of
some original tulip bulbs could have resulted as tulips
in general, and certain varieties in particular, became
fashionable. However, as the prized bulbs become
(45) more readily available through reproduction from the
original bulb, their price falls rapidly; after less than
30 years, bulbs sell at reproduction cost. But this
does not mean that the high prices of original bulbs
are irrational, for earnings derivable from the millions
(50) of bulbs descendent from the original bulbs can be
very high, even if each individual descendent bulb
commands a very low price. Given that an original
bulb can generate a reasonable return on investment
even if the price of descendent bulbs decreases
(55) dramatically, a rapid rise and eventual fall of tulip
bulb prices need not indicate a speculative bubble.

22.   Which one of the following most accurately expresses
the main point of the passage?

(A)   The seventeenth-century Dutch tulip market is
widely but mistakenly believed by economists
to provide an example of a speculative bubble.
(B)   Mackay did not accurately assess the earnings
that could be derived from rare and expensive
seventeenth-century Dutch tulip bulbs.
(C)   A speculative bubble occurs whenever the price
of an asset increases substantially followed by
a rapid and dramatic decline.
(D)   Garber argues that Mackay's classic account of
the seventeenth-century Dutch tulip market as
a speculative bubble is not supported by the
evidence.
(E)   A tulip bulb can generate a reasonable return on
investment even if the price starts very high
and decreases dramatically.

23.   Given Garber's account of the seventeenth-century
Dutch tulip market, which one of the following is most
analogous to someone who bought a tulip bulb of a
certain variety in that market at a very high price, only
to sell a bulb of that variety at a much lower price?

(A)   someone who, after learning that many others
had withdrawn their applications for a
particular job, applied for the job in the belief
that there would be less competition for it
(B)   an art dealer who, after paying a very high
price for a new painting, sells it at a very low
price because it is now considered to be an
inferior work
(C)   someone who, after buying a box of rare
motorcycle parts at a very high price, is forced
to sell them at a much lower price because of
the sudden availability of cheap substitute parts
(D)   a publisher who pays an extremely high price
for a new novel only to sell copies at a price
affordable to nearly everyone
(E)   an airline that, after selling most of the tickets
for seats on a plane at a very high price, must
sell the remaining tickets at a very low price

GO ON TO THE NEXT PAGE.

24. The passage most strongly supports the inference that Garber would agree with which one of the following statements?

    (A)   If speculative bubbles occur at all, they occur very rarely.
    (B)   Many of the owners of high-priced original tulip bulbs could have expected to at least recoup their original investments from sales of the many bulbs propagated from the original bulbs.
    (C)   If there is not a speculative bubble in a market, then the level of prices in that market is not irrational.
    (D)   Most people who invested in Dutch tulip bulbs in the seventeenth century were generally rational in all their investments.
    (E)   Mackay mistakenly infers from the fact that tulip prices dropped rapidly that the very low prices that the bulbs eventually sold for were irrational.

25. The passage states that Mackay claimed which one of the following?

    (A)   The rapid rise in price of Dutch tulip bulbs was not due to the fashionability of the flowers they produced.
    (B)   The prices of certain varieties of Dutch tulip bulbs during the seventeenth century were, at least for a time, determined by speculation.
    (C)   The Netherlands was the only center of cultivation and development of new tulip varieties in the seventeenth century.
    (D)   The very high prices of bulbs in the seventeenth-century Dutch tulip market were not irrational.
    (E)   Buyers of rare and very expensive Dutch tulip bulbs were ultimately able to derive earnings from bulbs descendent from the original bulbs.

26. The main purpose of the second paragraph is to

    (A)   present the facts that are accepted by all experts in the field
    (B)   identify the mistake that one scholar alleges another scholar made
    (C)   explain the basis on which one scholar makes an inference with which another scholar disagrees
    (D)   undermine the case that one scholar makes for the claim with which another scholar disagrees
    (E)   outline the factual errors that led one scholar to draw the inference that he drew

27. The phrase "standard pricing pattern" as used in line 38 most nearly means a pricing pattern

    (A)   against which other pricing patterns are to be measured
    (B)   that conforms to a commonly agreed-upon criterion
    (C)   that is merely acceptable
    (D)   that regularly recurs in certain types of cases
    (E)   that serves as an exemplar

S T O P

IF YOU FINISH BEFORE TIME IS CALLED, YOU MAY CHECK YOUR WORK ON THIS SECTION ONLY.
DO NOT WORK ON ANY OTHER SECTION IN THE TEST.

SECTION III

Time—35 minutes

25 Questions

<u>Directions:</u> The questions in this section are based on the reasoning contained in brief statements or passages. For some questions, more than one of the choices could conceivably answer the question. However, you are to choose the <u>best</u> answer; that is, the response that most accurately and completely answers the question. You should not make assumptions that are by commonsense standards implausible, superfluous, or incompatible with the passage. After you have chosen the best answer, blacken the corresponding space on your answer sheet.

1. Aristophanes' play *The Clouds*, which was written when the philosopher Socrates was in his mid-forties, portrays Socrates as an atheistic philosopher primarily concerned with issues in natural science. The only other surviving portrayals of Socrates were written after Socrates' death at age 70. They portrayed Socrates as having a religious dimension and a strong focus on ethical issues.

   Which one of the following, if true, would most help to resolve the apparent discrepancy between Aristophanes' portrayal of Socrates and the other surviving portrayals?

   (A) Aristophanes' portrayal of Socrates in *The Clouds* was unflattering, whereas the other portrayals were very flattering.
   (B) Socrates' philosophical views and interests changed sometime after his mid-forties.
   (C) Most of the philosophers who lived before Socrates were primarily concerned with natural science.
   (D) Socrates was a much more controversial figure in the years before his death than he was in his mid-forties.
   (E) Socrates had an influence on many subsequent philosophers who were primarily concerned with natural science.

2. Board member: The J Foundation, a philanthropic organization, gave you this grant on the condition that your resulting work not contain any material detrimental to the J Foundation's reputation. But your resulting work never mentions any of the laudable achievements of our foundation. Hence your work fails to meet the conditions under which the grant was made.

   The reasoning in the board member's argument is vulnerable to criticism on the grounds that the argument

   (A) takes for granted that a work that never mentions any laudable achievements cannot be of high intellectual value
   (B) confuses a condition necessary for the receipt of a grant with a condition sufficient for the receipt of a grant
   (C) presumes, without providing justification, that a work that does not mention a foundation's laudable achievements is harmful to that foundation's reputation
   (D) fails to consider that recipients of a grant usually strive to meet a foundation's conditions
   (E) fails to consider the possibility that the work that was produced with the aid of the grant may have met all conditions other than avoiding detriment to the J Foundation's reputation

3. Psychiatrist: Breaking any habit is difficult, especially when it involves an addictive substance. People who break a habit are more likely to be motivated by immediate concerns than by long-term ones. Therefore, people who succeed in breaking their addiction to smoking cigarettes are more likely to be motivated by the social pressure against smoking—which is an immediate concern—than by health concerns, since _____.

   The conclusion of the psychiatrist's argument is most strongly supported if which one of the following completes the argument?

   (A) a habit that involves an addictive substance is likely to pose a greater health threat than a habit that does not involve any addictive substance
   (B) for most people who successfully quit smoking, smoking does not create an immediate health concern at the time they quit
   (C) some courses of action that exacerbate health concerns can also relieve social pressure
   (D) most people who succeed in quitting smoking succeed only after several attempts
   (E) everyone who succeeds in quitting smoking is motivated either by social pressure or by health concerns

GO ON TO THE NEXT PAGE.

4. Cassie: In order to improve the quality of customer service provided by our real estate agency, we should reduce client loads—the number of clients each agent is expected to serve at one time.

Melvin: Although smaller client loads are desirable, reducing client loads at our agency is simply not feasible. We already find it very difficult to recruit enough qualified agents; recruiting even more agents, which would be necessary in order to reduce client loads, is out of the question.

Of the following, which one, if true, is the logically strongest counter that Cassie can make to Melvin's argument?

(A) Since reducing client loads would improve working conditions for agents, reducing client loads would help recruit additional qualified agents to the real estate agency.

(B) Many of the real estate agency's current clients have expressed strong support for efforts to reduce client loads.

(C) Several recently conducted studies of real estate agencies have shown that small client loads are strongly correlated with high customer satisfaction ratings.

(D) Hiring extra support staff for the real estate agency's main office would have many of the same beneficial effects as reducing client loads.

(E) Over the last several years, it has become increasingly challenging for the real estate agency to recruit enough qualified agents just to maintain current client loads.

5. The star-nosed mole has a nose that ends in a pair of several-pointed stars, or tentacles that are crucial for hunting, as moles are poor-sighted. These tentacles contain receptors that detect electric fields produced by other animals, enabling the moles to detect and catch suitable prey such as worms and insects.

Which one of the following is most strongly supported by the information above?

(A) Both worms and insects produce electric fields.

(B) The star-nosed mole does not rely at all on its eyesight for survival.

(C) The star-nosed mole does not rely at all on its sense of smell when hunting.

(D) Only animals that hunt have noses with tentacles that detect electric fields.

(E) The star-nosed mole does not produce an electric field.

6. In her recent book a psychologist described several cases that exhibit the following pattern: A child, denied something by its parent, initiates problematic behavior such as screaming; the behavior escalates until finally the exasperated parent acquiesces to the child's demand. At this point the child, having obtained the desired goal, stops the problematic behavior, to the parent's relief. This self-reinforcing pattern of misbehavior and accommodation is repeated with steadily increasing levels of misbehavior by the child.

The cases described by the psychologist illustrate each of the following generalizations EXCEPT:

(A) A child can develop problematic behavior patterns as a result of getting what it wants.

(B) A child and parent can mutually influence each other's behavior.

(C) Parents, by their choices, can inadvertently increase their child's level of misbehavior.

(D) A child can unintentionally influence a parent's behavior in ways contrary to the child's intended goals.

(E) A child can get what it wants by doing what its parent doesn't want it to do.

7. Scientist: In our study, chemical R did not cause cancer in laboratory rats. But we cannot conclude from this that chemical R is safe for humans. After all, many substances known to be carcinogenic to humans cause no cancer in rats; this is probably because some carcinogens cause cancer only via long-term exposure and rats are short lived.

Which one of the following most precisely describes the role played in the scientist's argument by the statement that chemical R did not cause cancer in laboratory rats?

(A) It is cited as evidence against the conclusion that chemical R is safe for humans.

(B) It is advanced to support the contention that test results obtained from laboratory rats cannot be extrapolated to humans.

(C) It illustrates the claim that rats are too short lived to be suitable as test subjects for the carcinogenic properties of substances to which humans are chronically exposed.

(D) It is used as evidence to support the hypothesis that chemical R causes cancer in humans via long-term exposure.

(E) It is cited as being insufficient to support the conclusion that chemical R is safe for humans.

GO ON TO THE NEXT PAGE.

8. Department store manager: There is absolutely no
    reason to offer our customers free gift wrapping
    again this holiday season. If most customers take
    the offer, it will be expensive and time-consuming
    for us. On the other hand, if only a few customers
    want it, there is no advantage in offering it.

    Which one of the following is an assumption required
    by the department store manager's argument?

    (A)   Gift wrapping would cost the store more during
          this holiday season than in previous holiday
          seasons.
    (B)   Anything that slows down shoppers during the
          holiday season costs the store money.
    (C)   It would be to the store's advantage to charge
          customers for gift wrapping services.
    (D)   It would be expensive to inform customers
          about the free gift wrapping service.
    (E)   Either few customers would want free gift
          wrapping or most customers would want it.

9. Among people who have a history of chronic trouble
    falling asleep, some rely only on sleeping pills to help
    them fall asleep, and others practice behavior
    modification techniques and do not take sleeping pills.
    Those who rely only on behavior modification fall
    asleep more quickly than do those who rely only on
    sleeping pills, so behavior modification is more effective
    than are sleeping pills in helping people to fall asleep.

    Which one of the following, if true, most weakens the
    argument?

    (A)   People who do not take sleeping pills spend at
          least as many total hours asleep each night as
          do the people who take sleeping pills.
    (B)   Most people who have trouble falling asleep
          and who use behavior modification techniques
          fall asleep more slowly than do most people
          who have no trouble falling asleep.
    (C)   Many people who use only behavior
          modification techniques to help them fall
          asleep have never used sleeping pills.
    (D)   The people who are the most likely to take
          sleeping pills rather than practice behavior
          modification techniques are those who have
          previously had the most trouble falling asleep.
    (E)   The people who are the most likely to practice
          behavior modification techniques rather than
          take sleeping pills are those who prefer not to
          use drugs if other treatments are available.

10. Lawyer: This witness acknowledges being present at the
    restaurant and watching when my client, a famous
    television personality, was assaulted. Yet the
    witness claims to recognize the assailant, but not
    my famous client. Therefore, the witness's
    testimony should be excluded.

    The lawyer's conclusion follows logically if which one
    of the following is assumed?

    (A)   If a witness claims to recognize both parties
          involved in an assault, then the witness's
          testimony should be included.
    (B)   There are other witnesses who can identify the
          lawyer's client as present during the assault.
    (C)   It is impossible to determine whether the
          witness actually recognized the assailant.
    (D)   The testimony of a witness to an assault should
          be included only if the witness claims to
          recognize both parties involved in the assault.
    (E)   It is unlikely that anyone would fail to
          recognize the lawyer's client.

11. Biologist: Many paleontologists have suggested that the
    difficulty of adapting to ice ages was responsible
    for the evolution of the human brain. But this
    suggestion must be rejected, for most other
    animal species adapted to ice ages with no
    evolutionary changes to their brains.

    The biologist's argument is most vulnerable to criticism
    on which one of the following grounds?

    (A)   It fails to address adequately the possibility that
          even if a condition is sufficient to produce an
          effect in a species, it may not be necessary to
          produce that effect in that species.
    (B)   It fails to address adequately the possibility that
          a condition can produce a change in a species
          even if it does not produce that change in
          other species.
    (C)   It overlooks the possibility that a condition that
          is needed to produce a change in one species
          is not needed to produce a similar change in
          other species.
    (D)   It presumes without warrant that human beings
          were presented with greater difficulties during
          ice ages than were individuals of most other
          species.
    (E)   It takes for granted that, if a condition
          coincided with the emergence of a certain
          phenomenon, that condition must have been
          causally responsible for the phenomenon.

GO ON TO THE NEXT PAGE.

12. The total number of book titles published annually in North America has approximately quadrupled since television first became available. Retail sales of new titles, as measured in copies, increased rapidly in the early days of television, though the rate of increase has slowed in recent years. Library circulation has been flat or declining in recent years.

Which one of the following is most strongly supported by the information above?

(A) Television has, over the years, brought about a reduction in the amount of per capita reading in North America.

(B) The introduction of television usually brings about a decrease in library use.

(C) Book publishers in North America now sell fewer copies per title than they sold in the early days of television.

(D) The availability of television does not always cause a decline in the annual number of book titles published or in the number of books sold.

(E) The introduction of television expanded the market for books in North America.

13. Botanist: It has long been believed that people with children or pets should keep poinsettia plants out of their homes. Although this belief has been encouraged by child-rearing books, which commonly list poinsettias as poisonous and therefore dangerous, it is mistaken. Our research has shown, conclusively, that poinsettias pose no risk to children or pets.

Which one of the following most accurately expresses the conclusion drawn in the botanist's argument?

(A) Child-rearing books should encourage people with children to put poinsettias in their homes.

(B) Poinsettias are not dangerously poisonous.

(C) According to many child-rearing books, poinsettias are dangerous.

(D) The belief that households with children or pets should not have poinsettias is mistaken.

(E) Poinsettias pose no risk to children or pets.

14. Archaeologist: An ancient stone building at our excavation site was composed of three kinds of stone—quartz, granite, and limestone. Of these, only limestone occurs naturally in the area. Most of the buildings at the site from the same time period had limestone as their only stone component, and most were human dwellings. Therefore, the building we are studying probably was not a dwelling.

Which one of the following, if true, would most strengthen the archaeologist's reasoning?

(A) Most of the buildings that were used as dwellings at the site were made, at least in part, of limestone.

(B) Most of the buildings at the site that were not dwellings were made, at least in part, from types of stone that do not occur naturally in the area.

(C) Most of the buildings that were built from stones not naturally occurring in the area were not built with both quartz and granite.

(D) Most of the buildings at the site were used as dwellings.

(E) No quartz has been discovered on the site other than that found in the building being studied.

GO ON TO THE NEXT PAGE.

15. Theodore will be able to file his tax return on time only in the event that he has an accountant prepare his tax return and the accountant does not ask Theodore for any additional documentation of his business expenses. If he does have an accountant prepare his return, the accountant will necessarily ask Theodore to provide this additional documentation. Therefore, Theodore will not be able to file on time.

The pattern of reasoning in which one of the following arguments most closely parallels the pattern of reasoning in the argument above?

(A) Given the demands of Timothy's job, his next free evening will occur next Friday. Since he spent a lot of money on his last evening out, he will probably decide to spend his next free evening at home. Therefore, Timothy will probably be at home next Friday evening.

(B) Tovah cannot attend the concert next week if she is away on business. If she misses that concert, she will not have another opportunity to attend a concert this month. Since she will be away on business, Tovah will not be able to attend a concert this month.

(C) Mark's children will not be content this weekend unless he lets them play video games some of the time. Mark will let them play video games, but only at times when he has no other activities planned. Therefore, unless Mark and his children take a break from planned activities, Mark's children will not be content this weekend.

(D) If Teresa is not seated in first class on her airline flight, she will be seated in business class. Therefore, since she cannot be seated in first class on that flight, she will necessarily be seated in business class.

(E) Susannah will have a relaxing vacation only if her children behave especially well and she does not start to suspect that they are planning some mischief. Since she will certainly start to suspect that they are planning some mischief if they behave especially well, Susannah's vacation cannot possibly be relaxing.

16. When a threat to life is common, as are automobile and industrial accidents, only unusual instances tend to be prominently reported by the news media. Instances of rare threats, such as product tampering, however, are seen as news by reporters and are universally reported in featured stories. People in general tend to estimate the risk of various threats by how frequently those threats come to their attention.

If the statements above are true, which one of the following is most strongly supported on the basis of them?

(A) Whether governmental action will be taken to lessen a common risk depends primarily on the prominence given to the risk by the news media.

(B) People tend to magnify the risk of a threat if the threat seems particularly dreadful or if those who would be affected have no control over it.

(C) Those who get their information primarily from the news media tend to overestimate the risk of uncommon threats relative to the risk of common threats.

(D) Reporters tend not to seek out information about long-range future threats but to concentrate their attention on the immediate past and future.

(E) The resources that are spent on avoiding product tampering are greater than the resources that are spent on avoiding threats that stem from the weather.

GO ON TO THE NEXT PAGE.

17. Real estate agent: Upon selling a home, the sellers are legally entitled to remove any items that are not permanent fixtures. Legally, large appliances like dishwashers are not permanent fixtures. However, since many prospective buyers of the home are likely to assume that large appliances in the home would be included with its purchase, sellers who will be keeping the appliances are morally obliged either to remove them before showing the home or to indicate in some other way that the appliances are not included.

Which one of the following principles, if valid, most helps to justify the real estate agent's argumentation?

(A) If a home's sellers will be keeping any belongings that prospective buyers of the home might assume would be included with the purchase of the home, the sellers are morally obliged to indicate clearly that those belongings are not included.

(B) A home's sellers are morally obliged to ensure that prospective buyers of the home do not assume that any large appliances are permanent fixtures in the home.

(C) A home's sellers are morally obliged to include with the sale of the home at least some of the appliances that are not permanent fixtures but were in the home when it was shown to prospective buyers.

(D) A home's sellers are morally obliged not to deliberately mislead any prospective buyers of their home about which belongings are included with the sale of the home and which are not.

(E) If a home's sellers have indicated in some way that a large appliance is included with the home's purchase, then they are morally obliged not to remove that appliance after showing the home.

18. Many parents rigorously organize their children's activities during playtime, thinking that doing so will enhance their children's cognitive development. But this belief is incorrect. To thoroughly structure a child's playtime and expect this to produce a creative and resourceful child would be like expecting a good novel to be produced by someone who was told exactly what the plot and characters must be.

The argument is most vulnerable to criticism on which one of the following grounds?

(A) It takes for granted that if something is conducive to a certain goal it cannot also be conducive to some other goal.

(B) It overlooks the possibility that many children enjoy rigorously organized playtime.

(C) It takes a necessary condition for something's enhancing a child's creativity and resourcefulness to be a sufficient condition for its doing so.

(D) It fails to consider the possibility that being able to write a good novel requires something more than creativity and resourcefulness.

(E) It fails to consider the possibility that something could enhance a child's overall cognitive development without enhancing the child's creativity and resourcefulness.

19. Bureaucrat: The primary, constant goal of an ideal bureaucracy is to define and classify all possible problems and set out regulations regarding each eventuality. Also, an ideal bureaucracy provides an appeal procedure for any complaint. If a complaint reveals an unanticipated problem, the regulations are expanded to cover the new issue, and for this reason an ideal bureaucracy will have an ever-expanding system of regulations.

Which one of the following is an assumption the bureaucrat's argument requires?

(A) An ideal bureaucracy will provide an appeal procedure for complaints even after it has defined and classified all possible problems and set out regulations regarding each eventuality.

(B) For each problem that an ideal bureaucracy has defined and classified, the bureaucracy has received at least one complaint revealing that problem.

(C) An ideal bureaucracy will never be permanently without complaints about problems that are not covered by that bureaucracy's regulations.

(D) An ideal bureaucracy can reach its primary goal if, but only if, its system of regulations is always expanding to cover problems that had not been anticipated.

(E) Any complaint that an ideal bureaucracy receives will reveal an unanticipated problem that the bureaucracy is capable of defining and classifying.

GO ON TO THE NEXT PAGE.

20. Scientists studying a common type of bacteria have discovered that most bacteria of that type are in hibernation at any given time. Some microbiologists have concluded from this that bacteria in general are usually in hibernation. This conclusion would be reasonable if all types of bacteria were rather similar. But, in fact, since bacteria are extremely diverse, it is unlikely that most types of bacteria hibernate regularly.

Which one of the following most accurately expresses the overall conclusion of the argument?

(A) Bacteria of most types are usually in hibernation.
(B) It is probably not true that most types of bacteria hibernate regularly.
(C) If bacteria are extremely diverse, it is unlikely that most types of bacteria hibernate regularly.
(D) The conclusion that bacteria in general are usually in hibernation would be reasonable if all types of bacteria were rather similar.
(E) It is likely that only one type of bacteria hibernates regularly.

21. Any student who is not required to hand in written homework based on the reading assignments in a course will not complete all of the reading assignments. Even highly motivated students will neglect their reading assignments if they are not required to hand in written homework. Therefore, if the students in a course are given several reading assignments and no written assignments, no student in that course will receive a high grade for the course.

The conclusion of the argument follows logically if which one of the following is assumed?

(A) No student who completes anything less than all of the reading assignments for a course will earn a high grade for that course.
(B) Any student who completes all of the reading and written assignments for a course will earn a high grade in that course.
(C) All highly motivated students who complete all of the reading assignments for a course will receive high grades for that course.
(D) If highly motivated students are required to hand in written homework on their reading assignments, then they will complete all of their reading assignments.
(E) Some highly motivated students will earn high grades in a course if they are required to hand in written homework on their reading assignments.

22. In a study, one group of volunteers was fed a high-protein, low-carbohydrate diet; another group was fed a low-protein, high-carbohydrate diet. Both diets contained the same number of calories, and each volunteer's diet prior to the experiment had contained moderate levels of proteins and carbohydrates. After ten days, those on the low-carbohydrate diet had lost more weight than those on the high-carbohydrate diet. Thus, the most effective way to lose body fat is to eat much protein and shun carbohydrates.

Which one of the following, if true, most weakens the argument above?

(A) A low-protein, high-carbohydrate diet causes the human body to retain water, the added weight of which largely compensates for the weight of any body fat lost, whereas a high-protein, low-carbohydrate diet does not.
(B) Many people who consume large quantities of protein nevertheless gain significant amounts of body fat.
(C) A high-protein, low-carbohydrate diet will often enable the human body to convert some body fat into muscle, without causing any significant overall weight loss.
(D) In the experiment, the volunteers on the high-carbohydrate diet engaged in regular exercise of a kind known to produce weight loss, and those on the low-carbohydrate diet did not.
(E) Many of the volunteers who had been on the low-carbohydrate diet eventually regained much of the weight they had lost on the diet after returning to their normal diets.

GO ON TO THE NEXT PAGE.

23. Essayist: Computers have the capacity to represent and to perform logical transformations on pieces of information. Since exactly the same applies to the human mind, the human mind is a type of computer.

The flawed pattern of reasoning in which one of the following most closely resembles the flawed pattern of reasoning in the essayist's argument?

(A) Often individual animals sacrifice their lives when the survival of their offspring or close relatives is threatened. It is probable, therefore, that there is a biological basis for the fact that human beings are similarly often willing to sacrifice their own well-being for the good of their community.

(B) In the plastic arts, such as sculpture or painting, no work can depend for its effectiveness upon a verbal narrative that explains it. Since the same can be said of poetry, we cannot consider this characteristic as a reasonable criterion for distinguishing the plastic arts from other arts.

(C) In any organism, the proper functioning of each component depends upon the proper functioning of every other component. Thus, communities belong to the category of organisms, since communities are invariably characterized by this same interdependence of components.

(D) Some vitamins require the presence in adequate amounts of some mineral in order to be fully beneficial to the body. Thus, since selenium is needed to make vitamin E fully active, anyone with a selenium deficiency will have a greater risk of contracting those diseases from which vitamin E provides some measure of protection.

(E) Friendship often involves obligations whose fulfillment can be painful or burdensome. The same can be said of various forms of cooperation that cannot strictly be called friendship. Thus cooperation, like friendship, can require that priority be given to goals other than mere self-interest.

24. It is popularly believed that a poem has whatever meaning is assigned to it by the reader. But objective evaluation of poetry is possible only if this popular belief is false; for the aesthetic value of a poem cannot be discussed unless it is possible for at least two readers to agree on the correct interpretation of the poem.

Which one of the following is an assumption required by the argument?

(A) Only if they find the same meaning in a poem can two people each judge that it has aesthetic value.

(B) If two readers agree about the meaning of a given poem, that ensures that an objective evaluation of the poem can be made.

(C) Discussion of a poem is possible only if it is false that a poem has whatever meaning is assigned to it by the reader.

(D) A given poem can be objectively evaluated only if the poem's aesthetic value can be discussed.

(E) Aesthetic evaluation of literature is best accomplished through discussion by more than two readers.

25. Dean: The mathematics department at our university has said that it should be given sole responsibility for teaching the course Statistics for the Social Sciences. But this course has no more mathematics in it than high school algebra does. The fact that a course has mathematics in it does not mean that it needs to be taught by a mathematics professor, any more than a course approaching its subject from a historical perspective must be taught by a history professor. Such demands by the mathematics department are therefore unjustified.

The dean's argument is most vulnerable to criticism on the grounds that it

(A) presumes, without providing justification, that expertise in a subject does not enable one to teach that subject well

(B) purports to refute a view by showing that one possible reason for that view is insufficient

(C) presumes, without providing justification, that most students are as knowledgeable about mathematics as they are about history

(D) fails to establish that mathematics professors are not capable of teaching Statistics for the Social Sciences effectively

(E) presumes, without providing justification, that any policies that apply to history courses must be justified with respect to mathematics courses

S T O P

IF YOU FINISH BEFORE TIME IS CALLED, YOU MAY CHECK YOUR WORK ON THIS SECTION ONLY.
DO NOT WORK ON ANY OTHER SECTION IN THE TEST.

SECTION IV

Time—35 minutes

23 Questions

<u>Directions:</u> Each group of questions in this section is based on a set of conditions. In answering some of the questions, it may be useful to draw a rough diagram. Choose the response that most accurately and completely answers each question and blacken the corresponding space on your answer sheet.

<u>Questions 1–6</u>

There are exactly six law students—Gambini, Little, Mitchum, Richardson, Saito, and Veracruz—in a trial advocacy class. The class is divided into three trial teams—team 1, team 2, and team 3—of exactly two students each. Each student is on exactly one of the teams. Each student prepares exactly one of either the opening argument or the final argument for his or her team. The teams must be formed according to the following specifications:

Mitchum is on the same team as either Gambini or Veracruz.

Little prepares an opening argument.

Either Gambini or Richardson, but not both, prepares a final argument.

1. Which one of the following could be the composition of each team and the argument each student prepares?

(A)   team 1: Little, opening; Gambini, final
       team 2: Veracruz, opening; Mitchum, final
       team 3: Saito, opening; Richardson, final
(B)   team 1: Mitchum, opening; Gambini, final
       team 2: Veracruz, opening; Little, final
       team 3: Richardson, opening; Saito, final
(C)   team 1: Richardson, opening; Gambini, final
       team 2: Mitchum, opening; Saito, final
       team 3: Little, opening; Veracruz, final
(D)   team 1: Gambini, opening; Mitchum, final
       team 2: Little, opening; Richardson, final
       team 3: Veracruz, opening; Saito, final
(E)   team 1: Gambini, opening; Mitchum, final
       team 2: Richardson, opening; Saito, final
       team 3: Little, opening; Veracruz, final

2. If Gambini is on the same team as Mitchum, and if Gambini prepares the final argument for that team, then which one of the following could be true?

(A)   Little is on the same team as Veracruz, who prepares the opening argument for the team.
(B)   Richardson is on the same team as Saito, who prepares the opening argument for the team.
(C)   Richardson is on the same team as Saito, who prepares the final argument for the team.
(D)   Saito is on the same team as Veracruz, who prepares the opening argument for the team.
(E)   Saito is on the same team as Veracruz, who prepares the final argument for the team.

3. Which one of the following could be true?

(A)   Gambini, who prepares a final argument, is on the same team as Richardson.
(B)   Gambini, who prepares a final argument, is on the same team as Veracruz.
(C)   Gambini, who prepares an opening argument, is on the same team as Little.
(D)   Little, who prepares an opening argument, is on the same team as Mitchum.
(E)   Mitchum, who prepares an opening argument, is on the same team as Saito.

4. If Richardson is on the same team as Veracruz, then for exactly how many of the students can it be determined which of the arguments he or she prepares?

(A)   one
(B)   two
(C)   three
(D)   four
(E)   five

5. If Little is on the same team as Richardson, then which one of the following must be true?

(A)   Saito is on the same team as Veracruz.
(B)   Gambini is on the same team as Mitchum.
(C)   Mitchum prepares a final argument.
(D)   Veracruz prepares a final argument.
(E)   Gambini prepares an opening argument.

6. If Saito prepares an opening argument, then which one of the following pairs of students could be on the same team as each other?

(A)   Gambini and Little
(B)   Gambini and Saito
(C)   Little and Veracruz
(D)   Mitchum and Veracruz
(E)   Richardson and Veracruz

GO ON TO THE NEXT PAGE.

Questions 7–12

While on vacation, Sukanya receives several e-mail messages from work, each message from one of three associates: Hilary, Jerome, and Lula. Sukanya receives at least one and no more than two messages from each of them. Sukanya receives each message on the day it is sent. No more than one message is sent each day. The messages are received in a manner consistent with the following:

The first message is not from Lula.
Both the first and last messages are from the same person.
Exactly once Sukanya receives a message from Jerome on the day after receiving one from Hilary.
Of the first three messages, exactly one is from Jerome.

7. Which one of the following could be an accurate list of the e-mail messages Sukanya receives, identified by the person each message is from and listed in the order she receives them?

(A) Lula, Hilary, Jerome, Hilary, Jerome, Lula
(B) Jerome, Lula, Hilary, Lula, Jerome
(C) Jerome, Lula, Hilary, Jerome, Hilary
(D) Jerome, Lula, Hilary, Hilary, Jerome
(E) Hilary, Lula, Lula, Jerome, Jerome, Hilary

8. What is the maximum possible number of e-mail messages Sukanya receives after Jerome's first message but before Hilary's first message?

(A) zero
(B) one
(C) two
(D) three
(E) four

9. If Sukanya receives exactly four e-mail messages, then which one of the following must be true?

(A) Exactly one of the messages is from Lula.
(B) Exactly two of the messages are from Jerome.
(C) The second message is from Lula.
(D) The third message is from Hilary.
(E) The fourth message is from Jerome.

10. Which one of the following e-mail messages CANNOT be from Lula?

(A) the second message
(B) the third message
(C) the fourth message
(D) the fifth message (if there is a fifth one)
(E) the sixth message (if there is a sixth one)

11. If Sukanya receives six e-mail messages, the fifth of which is from Lula, which one of the following must be true?

(A) The first message is from Jerome.
(B) The second message is from Lula.
(C) The third message is from Hilary.
(D) The fourth message is from Jerome.
(E) The sixth message is from Lula

12. If Sukanya receives two e-mail messages from Lula, what is the maximum possible number of e-mail messages Sukanya receives after Lula's first message but before Lula's last message?

(A) zero
(B) one
(C) two
(D) three
(E) four

GO ON TO THE NEXT PAGE.

Questions 13–18

Mercotek carried out a study to compare the productivity of its night shift with that of its day shift. Every week the company's six crews—F, G, H, R, S, and T—were ranked from first (most productive) to sixth (least productive). There were no ties. For any given week, either G and T were the two night-shift crews or else S and H were—the four other crews were the day-shift crews for that week. The following relationships held for every week of the study:

F is more productive than G.
R is more productive than S.
R is more productive than T.
S is more productive than H.
G is more productive than T.

13. Which one of the following could be an accurate ranking of all the crews, in order from first to sixth, for a given week of the study?

(A) F, G, T, R, S, H
(B) F, R, G, T, H, S
(C) G, R, T, S, H, F
(D) R, F, G, S, H, T
(E) R, S, H, T, F, G

14. If F is ranked third for a given week of the study, then which one of the following could also be true of that week?

(A) G ranks second.
(B) H ranks fourth.
(C) R ranks second.
(D) S ranks fourth.
(E) T ranks fourth.

15. Which one of the following CANNOT be the crew ranked fifth for any given week of the study?

(A) G
(B) H
(C) R
(D) S
(E) T

16. For any given week of the study, the ranking of all the crews is completely determined if which one of the following is true?

(A) F ranks second that week.
(B) G ranks fifth that week.
(C) H ranks third that week.
(D) R ranks third that week.
(E) S ranks third that week.

17. If the night-shift crews rank fifth and sixth for a given week of the study, then which one of the following could also be true of that week?

(A) G ranks fourth.
(B) H ranks fifth.
(C) R ranks third.
(D) S ranks fourth.
(E) T ranks fifth.

18. Which one of the following is a complete and accurate list of the crews that CANNOT be ranked third for any given week of the study?

(A) G, H, S
(B) R, T
(C) F, T
(D) G, T
(E) T

GO ON TO THE NEXT PAGE.

Questions 19–23

A shuttle van stops exactly four times—once at Fundy, once at Los Altos, once at Mineola, and once at Simcoe—not necessarily in that order. The van starts with exactly four passengers on board—Greg, Jasmine, Rosa, and Vijay—each of whom gets off at a different stop. The following conditions hold:

Los Altos is the first or second stop.

Rosa is still on board when the van reaches Mineola.

Jasmine is on board longer than Vijay.

If Jasmine is still on board when the van reaches Fundy, then Greg is still on board when the van reaches Simcoe; otherwise, Greg is not still on board when the van reaches Simcoe.

19. Which one of the following could be a complete and accurate matching of stops, listed in the order in which the van stops at them, to the passengers who get off at them?

(A) Los Altos: Greg
     Mineola: Vijay
     Fundy: Jasmine
     Simcoe: Rosa
(B) Simcoe: Vijay
     Mineola: Greg
     Fundy: Rosa
     Los Altos: Jasmine
(C) Los Altos: Jasmine
     Mineola: Vijay
     Fundy: Greg
     Simcoe: Rosa
(D) Los Altos: Rosa
     Mineola: Vijay
     Fundy: Jasmine
     Simcoe: Greg
(E) Los Altos: Vijay
     Fundy: Jasmine
     Mineola: Rosa
     Simcoe: Greg

20. If Mineola is the first stop, which one of the following is a complete and accurate list of the passengers who could possibly get off there?

(A) Rosa
(B) Greg, Rosa
(C) Greg, Vijay
(D) Greg, Rosa, Vijay
(E) Jasmine, Rosa, Vijay

21. If Fundy is the first stop, then which one of the following could accurately list the passengers in order from first to last off?

(A) Greg, Vijay, Jasmine, Rosa
(B) Rosa, Vijay, Greg, Jasmine
(C) Vijay, Greg, Rosa, Jasmine
(D) Vijay, Jasmine, Greg, Rosa
(E) Vijay, Rosa, Jasmine, Greg

22. Which one of the following must be true if Greg is still on board both when the van reaches Los Altos and when it reaches Simcoe, not necessarily in that order, assuming he is the second one off the van?

(A) Vijay is on board when the van reaches Simcoe.
(B) Vijay is on board when the van reaches Los Altos.
(C) Rosa is on board when the van reaches Simcoe.
(D) Rosa is on board when the van reaches Fundy.
(E) Jasmine is on board when the van reaches Mineola.

23. If Greg is not on board when the van reaches Simcoe, then which one of the following must be false?

(A) Greg is on board when the van reaches Fundy.
(B) Jasmine is on board when the van reaches Mineola.
(C) Rosa is on board when the van reaches Fundy.
(D) Vijay is on board when the van reaches Fundy.
(E) Vijay is on board when the van reaches Mineola.

S T O P

IF YOU FINISH BEFORE TIME IS CALLED, YOU MAY CHECK YOUR WORK ON THIS SECTION ONLY.
DO NOT WORK ON ANY OTHER SECTION IN THE TEST.

Wait for the supervisor's instructions before you open the page to the topic.
Please print and sign your name and write the date in the designated spaces below.

Time: 35 Minutes

General Directions

You will have 35 minutes in which to plan and write an essay on the topic inside. Read the topic and the accompanying directions carefully. You will probably find it best to spend a few minutes considering the topic and organizing your thoughts before you begin writing. In your essay, be sure to develop your ideas fully, leaving time, if possible, to review what you have written. **Do not write on a topic other than the one specified. Writing on a topic of your own choice is not acceptable.**

No special knowledge is required or expected for this writing exercise. Law schools are interested in the reasoning, clarity, organization, language usage, and writing mechanics displayed in your essay. How well you write is more important than how much you write.

Confine your essay to the blocked, lined area on the front and back of the separate Writing Sample Response Sheet. Only that area will be reproduced for law schools. Be sure that your writing is legible.

Both this topic sheet and your response sheet must be turned over to the testing staff before you leave the room.

LSAC ®

Topic Code	Print Your Full Name Here		
071292	Last	First	M.I.

Date	Sign Your Name Here
/ /	

Scratch Paper
Do not write your essay in this space.

LSAT® Writing Sample Topic

Directions: The scenario presented below describes two choices, either one of which can be supported on the basis of the information given. Your essay should consider both choices and argue for one over the other, based on the two specified criteria and the facts provided. There is no "right" or "wrong" choice: a reasonable argument can be made for either.

Aña Rodriguez is a shy five-year-old girl. The Rodriguez family must send Aña to either Mercer Preschool or Butte Preschool. The Rodriguezes are equally satisfied with the quality of the teachers and the facilities at both schools. Using the facts below, write an essay in which you argue for one preschool over the other based on the following two criteria:

- The preschool must provide a stimulating social environment for Aña.
- The preschool must be conveniently located.

Aña is an only child who lives on a block with no other children her age. Two children Aña occasionally plays with at the local playground would be in her class at Mercer. The class size at Mercer is eight children. Mercer occupies its students' time, for the most part, with activities for the entire class. There is little unstructured time. Mercer is within easy walking distance of the Rodriguez home. Parking near Mercer is nearly impossible. After the infrequent winter snowstorms, snow is typically left to melt rather than shoveled. Walking can be difficult at such times.

Aña's best friend will be attending Butte. Aña knows none of the other children who would be in her class. The class size at Butte is 12 children. Most of the students' time is not formally structured. The children are free to participate in a number of optional activities with or without their classmates. The few structured activities all involve small groups of two or three children. Butte is a 10-minute drive, or 20-minute bus ride from the Rodriguez house. Parking is always available since Butte has its own lot. Aña's younger cousin Pablo, who lives on her block, will be attending a different class at Butte.

WP-Q071A

Scratch Paper
Do not write your essay in this space.

Directions:

1. Use the Answer Key on the next page to check your answers.

2. Use the Scoring Worksheet below to compute your raw score.

3. Use the Score Conversion Chart to convert your raw score into the 120-180 scale.

Scoring Worksheet

1. Enter the number of questions you answered correctly in each section.

Number Correct

SECTION I. . . . . . _____
SECTION II . . . . . _____
SECTION III. . . . . _____
SECTION IV. . . . . _____

2. Enter the sum here: _____
   This is your Raw Score.

Conversion Chart
For Converting Raw Score to the 120-180 LSAT Scaled Score
LSAT Form 8LSN77

Reported Score	Raw Score Lowest	Raw Score Highest
180	99	100
179	98	98
178	97	97
177	96	96
176	—*	—*
175	95	95
174	94	94
173	—*	—*
172	93	93
171	92	92
170	91	91
169	90	90
168	89	89
167	87	88
166	86	86
165	85	85
164	83	84
163	82	82
162	81	81
161	79	80
160	77	78
159	76	76
158	74	75
157	72	73
156	70	71
155	69	69
154	67	68
153	65	66
152	63	64
151	61	62
150	59	60
149	58	58
148	56	57
147	54	55
146	52	53
145	50	51
144	48	49
143	47	47
142	45	46
141	43	44
140	41	42
139	40	40
138	38	39
137	36	37
136	35	35
135	33	34
134	32	32
133	30	31
132	29	29
131	27	28
130	26	26
129	25	25
128	24	24
127	22	23
126	21	21
125	20	20
124	19	19
123	18	18
122	17	17
121	16	16
120	0	15

*There is no raw score that will produce this scaled score for this form.

SECTION I

1.	B	8.	D	15.	D	22.	E
2.	A	9.	D	16.	B	23.	B
3.	C	10.	B	17.	D	24.	D
4.	A	11.	E	18.	E	25.	C
5.	B	12.	C	19.	C		
6.	A	13.	D	20.	A		
7.	A	14.	E	21.	B		

SECTION II

1.	D	8.	E	15.	D	22.	D
2.	A	9.	B	16.	C	23.	D
3.	A	10.	E	17.	B	24.	B
4.	B	11.	A	18.	C	25.	B
5.	E	12.	C	19.	D	26.	C
6.	E	13.	A	20.	B	27.	D
7.	A	14.	A	21.	A		

SECTION III

1.	B	8.	E	15.	E	22.	A
2.	C	9.	D	16.	C	23.	C
3.	B	10.	D	17.	A	24.	D
4.	A	11.	B	18.	E	25.	B
5.	A	12.	D	19.	C		
6.	D	13.	D	20.	B		
7.	E	14.	B	21.	A		

SECTION IV

1.	D	8.	C	15.	C	22.	C
2.	C	9.	A	16.	C	23.	D
3.	A	10.	E	17.	C		
4.	B	11.	D	18.	E		
5.	E	12.	B	19.	E		
6.	C	13.	D	20.	D		
7.	D	14.	B	21.	D		

LSAT® Prep Tools

LSAT ItemWise®

Get to know the LSAT

LSAC's popular, online LSAT familiarization tool, *LSAT ItemWise*:

- includes all three types of LSAT questions—logical reasoning, analytical reasoning, and reading comprehension;

- keeps track of your answers; and

- shows you explanations as to why answers are correct or incorrect.

Although it is best to use our paper-and-pencil *Official LSAT PrepTest®* products to fully prepare for the LSAT, you can enhance your preparation by understanding all three question types and why your answers are right or wrong.

ItemWise includes an introduction to the new reading comprehension question type—comparative reading—with sample questions and explanations.

LSAC account holders get unlimited online access to *ItemWise* for the length of the account.

$18 (at *www.LSAC.org*)